Every-Day Cookery,

Table Talk,

AND

Hints for the Laundry.

BY JULIET CORSON.

CHICAGO:
THE ADAMS & WESTLAKE MANUFACTURING CO.,
PUBLISHERS.
1884.

INGERSOLL & MARSH, PRINTERS, 170 CLARK ST., CHICAGO.

INDEX TO ADVERTISEMENTS.

The following advertisements appearing in this publication are of REPRESENTATIVE HOUSES *in their lines.*

LICENSED UNDER THE MITCHELL PATENT.

No. 1 *or* ONE-BURNER STOVE.

The No. 1 Stove is adapted for light work, such as heating a single sad-iron, heating water in the sick chamber, steeping tea and coffee, heating glue-pots, etc., etc.

N. B.—No attachments made for the No. 1.

A. & W. STOVE No. 2.

With NEW Sad-Heater Attachment. The No. 2 Sad Heater holds 3 irons by placing one on top. No. 3 attachment is larger. The sad-irons rest on a cast plate, which protects their face from the moist heat, and from smoke if flame is turned too high.

LICENSED UNDER THE MITCHELL PATENT.

No. 2 STOVE.

Cut showing Open Chimney Fronts, Open Hinge, Drum Removable, Patent Air Box, and Adjustable Wick Tubes.

A. & W. STOVE No. 2.

With Removable Extension Top, which affords room for 2 large and 2 small vessels.

LICENSED UNDER THE MITCHELL PATENT.

A. & W. STOVE, No. 3.

With Removable Extension Top and Oven.

LICENSED UNDER THE MITCHELL PATENT.

A. & W. STOVE No. 3. AND STAND.

No. 2 Stand, Same Style, Smaller.

These Stands are nicely Japanned and ornamented, and can be shipped in knock down.

LICENSED UNDER THE MITCHELL PATENT

A. & W. STOVE No. 3.

With Flue Heater Attachment. The same attachment is made for C and A Lamps, and for No. 2 Stove. The last two are smaller, and round instead of oblong.

The heat generated by the flame is discharged into this drum, which affords a considerable heating surface.

The flues, when they become warm, form a current, constantly drawing in cold air, which is heated while passing through; thus we have not only greater heating surface, but the additional advantage of changing the air by means of this current.

The No. 2 will heat any ordinary room fifteen feet square, and the No. 3, eighteen to twenty feet square.

The "A" Lamp and Heater is same capacity as the No. 2.

The "C" Lamp and Heater same as No. 3.

LICENSED UNDER THE MITCHELL PATENT.

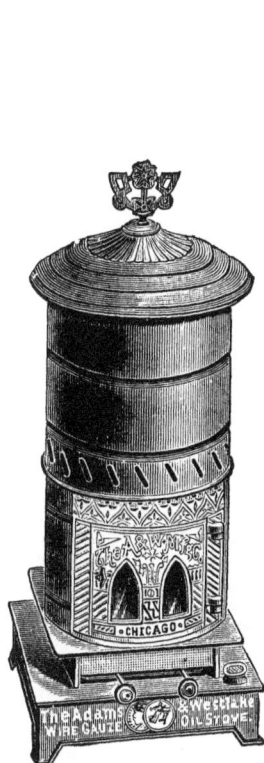 

No. 20.   No. 30.

A. & W. HEATING STOVES.

For Heating Purposes Only. Can be converted into Cook Stoves by
the addition of Cook Drums.

·No. **20** will heat a room 10 x 12 feet comfortably in the coldest weather. Top is
adjustable, so that a kettle of water may be heated quickly. Requires No. 2
Cook Drum to convert into a cook stove. *Dimensions*—Base, 10 x 10 inches;
height, 24 inches. Holds two quarts oil; will burn eight to ten hours.

No. **30.** More elaborate in design and finish, and much greater heating capacity
than our No. 20. The most powerful Oil Heating Stove made. As in our
No. 20, top may be removed and water heated. *Dimensions*—Base, 11 x 14½
inches; height, 30 inches. Holds about six quarts oil, which will burn fifteen
to eighteen hours. Requires No. 3 Cook Drum to convert into a cook stove.

THE WIRE-GAUZE WICK POCKETS.

Used in the A. & W. Stoves *only*, and on the same principle as the Sir Humphrey Davy Safety Lamp, making the Stove *absolutely non-explosive*, are attached INSIDE the reservoir, directly beneath the wick tubes.   With a small pocket of same material around and *inside* the place for filling, it is *impossible* for a flame to communicate with the oil or gas inside the reservoir ; therefore *there can be no explosion.*

CUT SHOWING CONSTRUCTION OF THE A. & W. OVEN.

Made with a *lining across the top and part way down the sides*, with openings for ventilation in the *top of the outer casing.*

This is without exception the *best baker* ever used on Oil or Gasoline Stoves, and is equal to any Range or Cook Stove.

SIZES. (Inside Measurement.)

A. & W. Oven,   10 wide, 15 deep, 11½ high.
No. 42 Oven,   23 "   13 "   18   "
Monarch "A" Oven, 12½ "   18 "   12   "

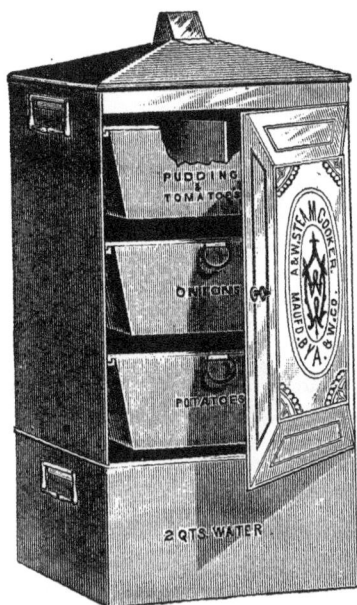

A. & W. STEAM COOKER.

Size, 10 x 10, three 3-qt. pans, which are made to slide out. Flat or pit copper bottom. For use on any Oil, Gas, Gasoline, Coal Stove or Range.

Cooking by steam, the best and purest heat known for the purpose ; saves time, space, labor and fuel.

Cooks four or five different articles at the same time without imparting the flavor of any to the other. Cabbage, onions, or fish may be cooked at the same time with rice, custard, etc., and none will in the least taste of the other.

Cooks meat, fowls, etc., perfectly tender in much less time than in the usual way, besides *retaining all their juices.* Rice, corn starch, oat meal, milk, pudding, etc., cooked with no possibility of burning.

Keeps food hot and perfectly fresh for hours without spoiling its flavor or drying it up.

THE "HANDY" COOKER.

For use on any Oil, Gas, Gasoline, Coal Stove or Range. Size, 10 x 10, four 3-pt. pails. Made either flat or pit copper bottom.

As shown by cut, four small pans or pails provided with short legs are made to stand inside the large vessel, sufficient space being allowed for water under and around them to cook food quickly and without danger of burning.

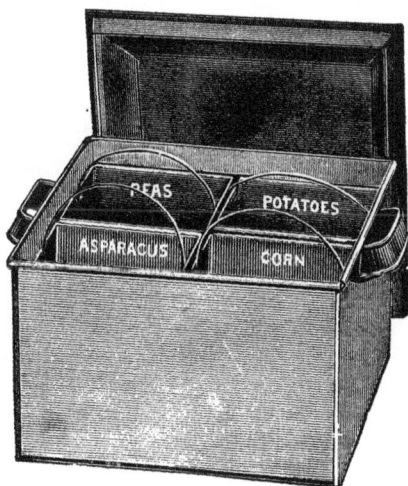

"A" LAMP.

With Flue Heater Attachment.

A. & W. WAFFLE IRON.

For Oil, Gas, Gasoline, Coal or Wood Stoves.

Reducing Ring for No. 3 Stove.

With this Ring, the oven or vessel may be used
directly over the stove without the
use of Extension Top.

Oyster Stew Pan.

Made expressly for the A. & W.
Oil Stoves, Nos. 1 and 2.

THE A. & W. PATENT BROILER.

Sold only with the A. & W. Stoves. With this broiler, the juices of the meat are retained, not lost, as in the usual method. There can be no singeing of meats, nor drippings to soil the stove.

During the five years we have sold this broiler with our stove, it has given entire satisfaction.

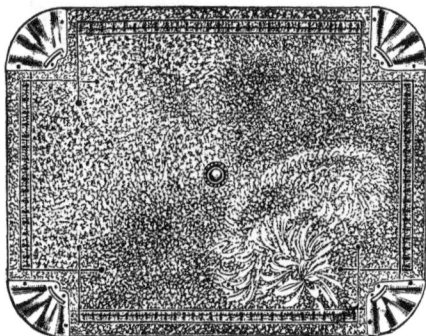

THE A. & W. "CRYSTAL" BOARD FOR OIL STOVES.

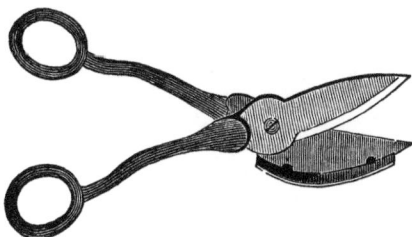

WICK TRIMMERS.

LICENSED UNDER THE MITCHELL PATENT.

A. & W. MONARCH "A" STOVE, 1883 (Oil).

Lamps removable by sliding out.   Boiling and baking done at the same time and with the same heat, as in Monarch "A," 1884.   Oven not removable.

The Warming Closet an important feature.

This Stove was a great success in 1883.

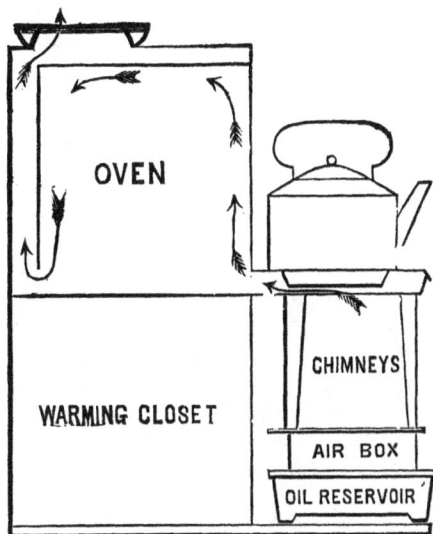

SECTIONAL VIEW OF

A. & W. MONARCH "A" STOVE, 1883.

The course of the heat, as shown by arrows, is first under the vessels, then into the oven, where it circulates freely, escaping finally through the passage at back of oven.

The Monarch "A," 1884, is made with Removable Oven.

LICENSED UNDER THE MITCHELL PATENT.

A. & W. MONARCH "A," 1884 (Oil).
INTERCHANGEABLE.

Mounted on Stand with Castors. Entire Stove, except Oven and Warming Closet, made in open work cast iron. Oven removable. Stove interchangeable with gasoline and gas.

Side and front bracket shelves are simply hooked on, and may be removed in an instant. The Warming Closet and Sliding Lamps are important features.

There is no other Oil Stove made on which such a variety or amount of cooking can be done at one and the same time. It will do as much work in a specified time *as any six-burner Stove made.*

For other illustrations of this Stove, see pages 17, 18 and 19.

For illustrations showing Monarch "A" changed into Gasoline Stove No. 40, see pages 26, 27 and 28, and to Gas Stove No. 56, pages 32 and 33.

LICENSED UNDER THE MITCHELL PATENT.

A. & W. MONARCH "A," 1884 (Oil).

INTERCHANGEABLE.

Showing Lamps in sliding frames, which support them in front of Stove when drawn out.

This is one of our many improvements for 1884, and will be found very convenient to fill the lamps, trim the wicks, heat sad-irons, boil or broil, when the use of the entire stove is not necessary.

The Lamps are provided with little handles (by oversight not shown in cuts) with which to lift them out of the sliding frames.

LICENSED UNDER THE MITCHELL PATENT.

A. & W. MONARCH "A," 1884 (Oil).

INTERCHANGEABLE.

WITHOUT STAND OR OVEN.

The Oven may be placed directly over the lamps if desired, but when placed at the back, as shown on pages 16 and 19, will bake or roast to perfection.

When the Oven is not used, the rear holes receive heat enough to boil water.

LICENSED UNDER THE MITCHELL PATENT.

A. & W. MONARCH "A," 1884 (Oil), AND OVEN.

INTERCHANGEABLE.

As shown in cut, the Monarch "A" is complete without the stand, and may be placed on a box or table.   The stand is secured to the stove by means of four little bolts, and is readily removed or attached.

LICENSED UNDER THE MITCHELL PATENT.

A. & W. MONARCH "C" (Oil).

INTERCHANGEABLE.

With Patent Top and Sliding Covers, adjusted for three vessels. Direct heat under middle one, over which the oven may be placed if desired.

The Lamp slides out, and is complete in itself.

LICENSED UNDER THE MITCHELL PATENT.

A. & W. MONARCH "C" (Oil).

INTERCHANGEABLE.

With Patent Top, sliding covers drawn out, making a four-holed top. By simply removing the center piece and sliding the end covers together, a hole is formed in the center for direct heat. (See other cuts.) These sliding covers are so arranged that they cannot fall off or tip.

By leaving the sliding covers drawn out, when the center piece is removed, an ordinary No. 8 Wash Boiler (pit or flat bottom) will fit directly over the flames.

LICENSED UNDER THE MITCHELL PATENT.

A. & W. MONARCH "C" (Oil) AND OVEN.

INTERCHANGEABLE.

The side shelves are simply hooked on, and may be removed at pleasure.

For other illustrations of this stove, see pages 20 and 21. For cuts showing the Monarch "C" changed to Gasoline Stove No. 41, see pages 23, 24 and 25.

A. & W. MONARCH No. 41 (Gasoline) AND OVEN.

INTERCHANGEABLE.

The *only* Gasoline Stove having an *Extension* Top. All surplus heat is utilized, giving to our Two-Burner Stove greater capacity than any Three-Burner stove made, and at a saving of 33⅓ % in fuel.

Attachments same as for Monarch "C" and used in same manner. See page 22. For other illustrations of the No. 41 Gasoline Stove, see pages 24 and 25.

A. & W. MONARCH, No. 41 (Gasoline).

INTERCHANGEABLE.

A. & W. MONARCH No. 41 (Gasoline)
INTERCHANGEABLE.

For cuts showing the No. 41 changed to Monarch "C" (Oil), see pages 20, 21 and 22.

A. & W. MONARCH No. 40 (Gasoline).

(OVEN PUT AWAY.)

INTERCHANGEABLE.

For other illustrations of this Stove, see pages 27 and 28.
For cuts showing No. 40 changed to Monarch "A" (Oil), see pages 16 and 17, and to Gas Stove No. 56, see pages 32 and 33.

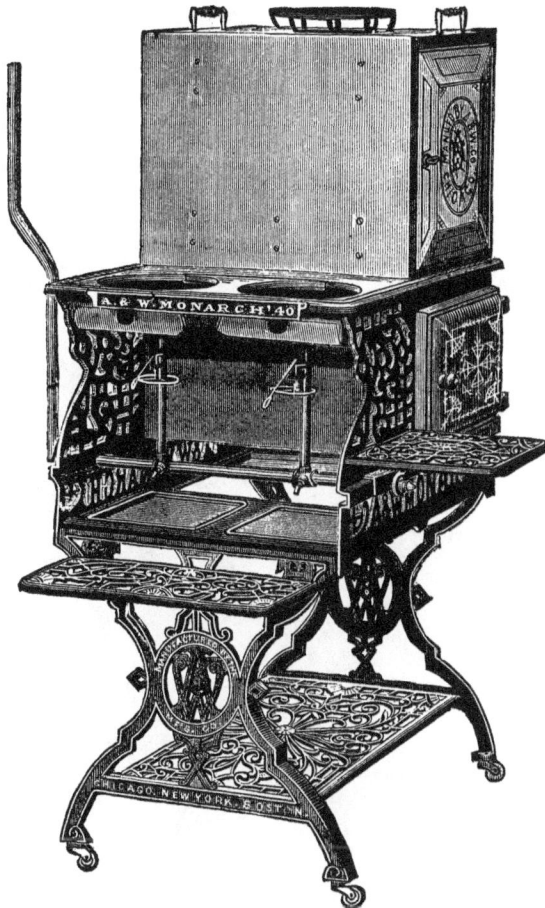

A. & W. MONARCH No. 40 (Gasoline).

INTERCHANGEABLE.

The most complete Gasoline Stove made. Arranged to receive one or two extra burners when desired. See page 28.

The only Gasoline Stove that will boil and bake at the same time and with the same heat, and the only one made with a Warming Closet.

A. & W. MONARCH No. 40 (Gasoline),

WITH EXTENSION BURNER.

INTERCHANGEABLE.

This extra Burner can be added at any time, if found desirable.   The heat from the extra Burner does not communicate with the oven.

A. & W. GASOLINE STOVE No. 42.

WITH A. & W. GASOLINE BURNERS.

Back and end shelf abjustable. Each Stove adapted for an extra Burner, thus readily converting it into a four-hole Stove when desired.

TANK.

Used on all A. & W. Gasoline Stoves. With
Regulating Supply Valve and
Indicator Float.

Top being concave, any fluid that may be
spilled in filling will run
into the Tank.

Made of heavy Tin, and finished in Bronze.

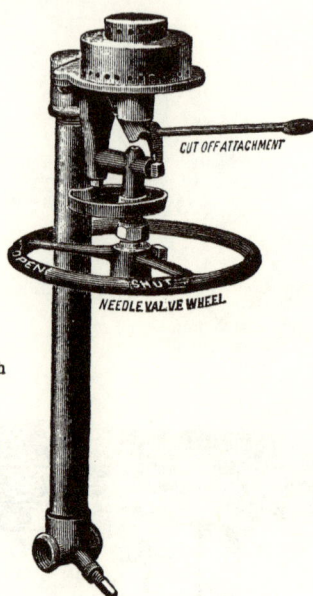

THE A. & W. BURNER.

USED ON ALL THE A. & W. GASOLINE STOVES.

SIMPLE AND PERFECT!

The *vertical* needle valve is opened and closed by simply a *five-eighth* turn of
the large wheel, the two spokes of which act as stops when the valve is entirely
closed or entirely open.

Each burner is supplied with a *cut-off attachment,* a most important feature, as
by it a small, strong flame may be maintained at slight cost, thus keeping the stove
ready for instant use. Another important advantage of this attachment will be
appreciated by those familiar with ordinary Gasoline Stoves. On first lighting
them, it requires some time to generate sufficient gas to maintain a strong flame,
and a slight puff of wind will blow it out; but by using the cut-off, the gas is all
concentrated into one *small, strong jet,* which will ignite before the *small* amount
of gasoline needed in the cup is consumed.

The flame is carried from the cut-off to the burner cap by simply throwing
down the cut-off lever, and from the cap to the cut-off by throwing it up.

THE A. & W.   GAS STOVES.

No. 52.

RUSSIA IRON BODIES.   CASTINGS JAPANNED.

No. 50.   No. 51.

NO. 54 GAS STOVE, WITH THE A. & W. GAS BURNER.

This Stove works to perfection, and is the cheapest Gas Stove for the money on the market.

Extension Top, and other attachments for No. 2 Oil Stove are adapted to this Stove.

A. & W. MONARCH No. 56 (Gas).

(OVEN PUT AWAY.)

INTERCHANGEABLE.

For another illustration of this Stove, see page 33.

For cuts showing No. 56 changed to Monarch "A" (Oil), see pages 16, 17, 18 and 19, and to No. 40 (Gasoline), pages 26, 27 and 28.

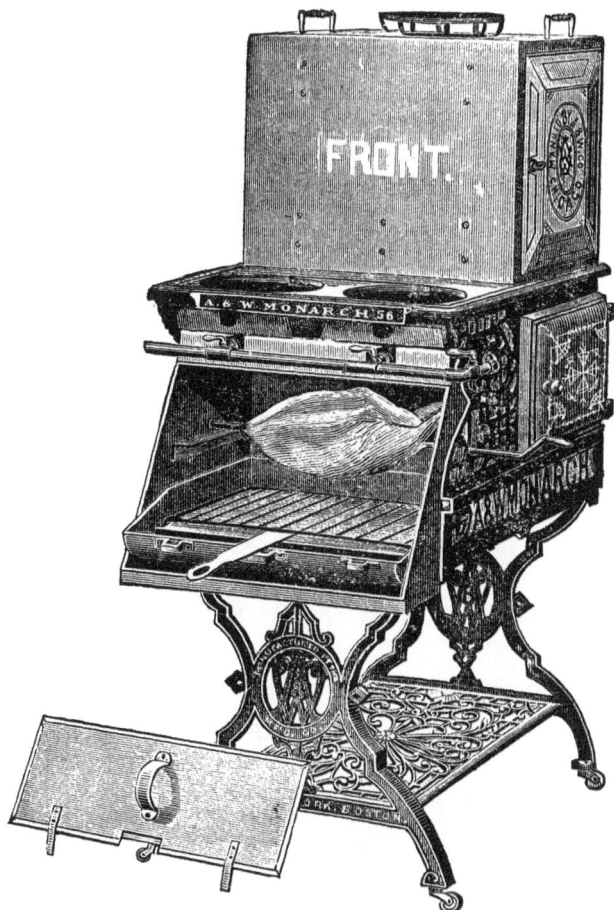

A. & W. MONARCH No. 56 (Gas).

(SHOWING PROCESS OF "SPITTING" A TURKEY.   OTHER FOWLS OR MEATS MAY BE
SERVED IN SAME MANNER.)

INTERCHANGEABLE.

The most complete and desirable *Gas Stove* on the market.

As shown in cuts, either Roasting, Spitting or Broiling may be done by means of a set of independent burners beneath the stove proper and in front of Warming Closet, while Boiling and Baking are being done above.   The Dripping Pan may be raised or lowered, as desired, and is provided with a trough, into which the juices of the meats run, where they are convenient for "basting" purposes.

Gas Burner used in Stoves Nos. 54 and 56.

Constructed so as to admit and mix air with the gas in the Burners.

Interchangeable.

Too much importance cannot be attached to the *Interchangeable* feature of the A. & W. *Monarch Stoves.*

These Stoves can *readily* be converted from an *Oil* to a *Gas* or *Gasoline* Stove, or vice versa.

This is important to the housekeeper, and of equal importance to the dealer:—to the former, as any one fuel, for some unforeseen cause, may become too expensive, or for a hundred and one reasons a change may be desired; to the latter, because he can fill from his stock orders for either kind of Stove by simply changing the fittings, which can be done in a few minutes by any one ordinarily skilled in the use of a wrench.

Capacity.

No. 1 Stove holds about three pints of oil, which will burn ten to twelve hours.

No. 2 Stove holds two quarts of oil, which will last, when burning full capacity, eight hours.

No. 3 Stove holds six quarts of oil, which will last from sixteen to eighteen hours.

No. 20 Heating Stove holds and consumes same quantity of oil as No. 2, and No. 30 same as No. 3.

The "C" Lamp holds four quarts of oil, which will last from ten to twelve hours, and the "A" Lamp two quarts, which will last eight hours.

Gasoline Tank holds nine pints, which will last in a One-Burner Stove, twenty-four hours or more; Two-Burner Stove, twelve to fourteen hours; Three-Burner Stove, eight to ten hours.

Finish.

The Nos. 1, 2 and 3 Stoves, also "A" and "C" Lamps, have NICKEL PLATED FRONTS, *handsomely designed.* The reservoirs are cast iron, galvanized inside and out, thoroughly oil tight, beautifully finished and ornamented.

With a solid crown plate, we are enabled to dispense with mica in chimneys, thus making it more convenient to light and no trouble to keep clean and in repair.

The stands and open work castings of all the A. & W. Stoves are nicely japanned and ornamented.

Gasoline.

The fact should not be lost sight of that Gasoline is dangerous, if *carelessly* or *improperly* handled.

It is very important that great care should be taken to procure the *best.*

Different grades of Gasoline are known by their degrees of gravity, and range from 63° to 90°.

PURE *Gasoline* of 74° is the *only grade* we can recommend. Its purity may be ascertained in the following manner: Pour three or four tablespoonfuls into a white saucer ; light it and let it burn entirely away.   If pure, there will be no residuum ; if impure, or of bad quality, a heavy, black substance will be found in bottom of saucer.

Dealers, as well as consumers, should be very careful as to storing Gasoline.   It should not be kept in a room where there is a fire, gas jet, lamp, or other artificial light, or where *children* can meddle with it.

Weights and Dimensions of Stoves.

		LBS.
No. 2 Stove only, ... Boxed,		35
No. 2 " including Top, Oven, Sad-Heater and Broiler, "		90
No. 3 Stove only, ... "		50
No. 3 " including Top, Oven, Sad-Heater and Broiler, "		105
Monarch "A" Stove, 1883, including Lamps, ... "		135
Monarch "A" " 1884, " " and Oven, . "		175
Monarch "A" " 1884, " " Oven and Stand, "		230
Monarch No. 40 Stove, including Oven and Stand, . . . "		165
Monarch No. 56 " " " " . . . "		165
Monarch " C " Stove, including Lamp and Oven, . . . "		145
Monarch No. 41 Stove, including Oven, ... "		125
No. 20 Stove, ... "		50
No. 30 " . . . . "		75
No. 42 " . . . . Crated,		95

	HEIGHT.	TOP OF STOVE.
Monarch "A," Nos. 40 and 56, ...	33 in.	21x25 in.
Monarch " C " and No. 41, ...	33 in.	13x38 in., ext'd.
Monarch " C " and No. 41, ...	33 in.	13x28 in., closed.
No. 42 Stove, including end and back shelf,	28 in.	21x54 in.

THE "DAISY" GLASS OIL CAN.

The *Glass Jar* is thoroughly protected by a Tin Jacket and Bottom, and the Glass cannot break.

THE CONTENTS CAN ALWAYS BE SEEN.

The "Daisy" is the only perfect Glass Oil Can made. Buy no other.

Three sizes :—½, 1 and 2 gallons.

THE "LITTLE JOKER"
FAMILY KEROSENE CAN AND PUMP.

Beats everything in the market.

Has Pump and adjustable Metal Spout, and all vessels can be readily filled.

Buy your oil in quantities and

SAVE MONEY.

Made of Heavy Tin, nicely painted, and will last for years.

Three sizes :—5, 10 and 20 gallons.

JUST THE THING FOR WEDDING, BIRTHDAY AND

HOLIDAY PRESENTS.

The Adams & Westlake Student Lamps.

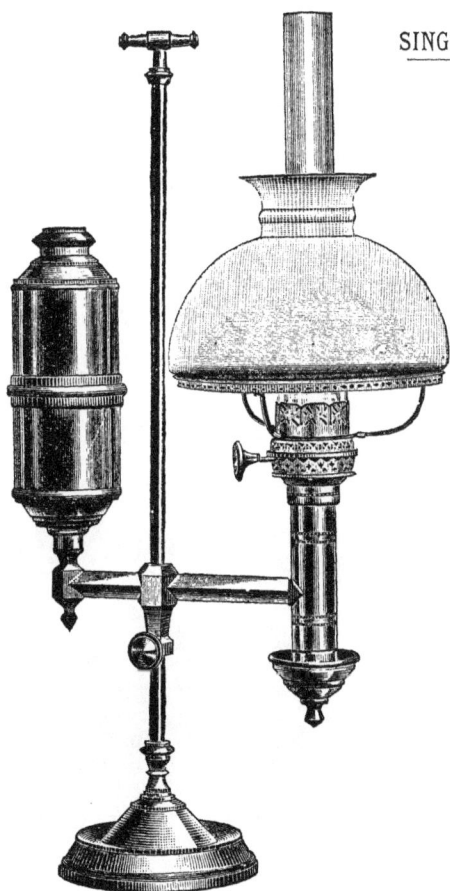

SINGLE AND DOUBLE BURNERS.

Of elegant design, beautifully finished.

The burner is the best made and *cannot get out of order.*

The wicks do not require any tying with thread to be kept in place, as in other Lamps.

BRASS & NICKEL PLATED.

The Double Burner Lamps have same pattern as Single Burner (see cut), and produce a steady and very powerful light.

Send for Price List and Circular, showing our

PATENT VALVE.

SOMETHING NEW!

THE

"PRETTY PEGGY" FLOUR SIFTER.

For sifting flour and meal ; for measuring, weighing, mixing, dredging and straining flour, meal, fruit and vegetables of all kinds.

This Sifter does not throw the flour over the sides, as others do.

When buying, see that the label has this cut, *printed in colors.*

BUY THE "PRETTY PEGGY."

SAVE YOUR CARPETS

BY USING THE

"PROTECTION" CUSPIDORS.

These Cuspidors are attached to a Mat 12 inches in diameter, and can be removed for cleaning.

If you miss the Cuspidor, you will

HIT THE MAT.

Made of Tin, Brass, Nickel, Bronze, Terra Cotta, Porcelain and Majolica.

Also made with

UMBRELLA RESTS.

PART FIRST.

EVERY-DAY COOKERY.

INTRODUCTORY.

THERE was a time, not many years ago, when the very root of our national prosperity, our liberal system of public education, threatened to exterminate from among us the dear old type of housewife. Our daughters, graduating from high-schools and seminaries, were too highly polished for every-day wear. But all that is changing now. The leading educational institutions are fast adding departments of domestic science to their regular routine of studies and accomplishments, and in many of them the pupils receive actual training in the practical branches of household economy. No other new departure in education was ever more welcome to the people than this, or more promising in its bearing upon society, for its effects reach everywhere, from the highest to the lowliest fireside in the land.

It is within the last decade that we have reconsidered one habit, which had come with our advancing prosperity and culture, that of leaving the treatment of our food supplies to untrained domestics. The home training of the daughters of a family was limited by circumstances; many mothers who had worked hard in their own youth thought they loved their daughters too well to make domestic drudges of them; others, who from choice deferred the inculcation of a knowledge of household matters until after the desired degree of intellectual culture had been secured, saw their girls step from the school-room to the management of a family, without having acquired any practical knowledge to guide them. Too often the influence of a literary education was a disdainful disregard for every-day usefulness. But, happily, those shining exceptions, women graced with both mental culture and domestic experience, are in the ascendency. No woman now is deemed "too bright or good for human nature's daily food"-preparation, or at least for an intelligent understanding of it.

We begin to realize that to a great extent a man's food makes or mars him. Both the brain and hand workers of the next generation will be ail the wiser and stronger for the attention the daily fare of their progenitors now receives. If cookery now commands intelligent investigation, it is because it no longer serves only the purposes of luxury, but has taken its proper place as an important factor in the scheme of social science. Now it is the pride of the accomplished and cultured woman to understand the practical working of every part of her household machinery, and to be able to guide it all personally.

CHAPTER I.

EFFECT OF COOKERY ON MEAT.

THERE is no reason why ordinary cooks should not understand something about the chemistry of cooking. There is seldom one so obtuse that she does not know the difference, by taste at least, between a good and a bad dinner. That difference once established in her mind, the task of making her comprehend why one way of cooking a meal makes it bad, while another makes it good, will not be a hopeless one. Facts are such stubborn things as to be capable of overcoming even stupidity, and any degree of ignorance save the willful.

If the fact can be demonstrated to a cook that tough meat can be made tender by softening the fibres with the action of a little vinegar, there will be no good reason why she should thereafter send a tough steak to the table. If she can be convinced that it is better to turn it over on a plate containing a little vinegar, salad oil, and pepper, four or five times in a couple of hours, instead of trying to make it tender by battering it with a rolling pin or cleaver, and so forcing out all its juices, she must be obstinate indeed if she still prefers the latter method, and the sooner her services are dispensed with the better for the temper and the digestion of her employer.

If a cook has not sufficient intelligence to master such knowledge for herself, there is no reason why her mistress should not acquire it, and impart it to her in a simplified form.

The effect of all cookery on food is the softening of its solid parts, the extraction of its juices and flavors and their judicious admixture, and the accomplishment of such chemical changes in its elements as are necessary before it can meet the requirements of the body. Cookery economizes food by these changes so that it yields the greatest degree of nourishment, and also presents a greater volume to the action of the digestive organs. That method of cooking is the most wholesome which prepares food most perfectly for the process of digestion, and presents the desired bulk in relation to the degree of nutriment it affords. Premising that the different operations in cooking meat are carefully performed, let us see which best accomplishes the desired result.

Meat loses about thirty per cent. of its bulk and juice in cooking, but it is thus prepared for mastication and digestion.

Broiled and roasted meat retains nearly all its juices, but loses about one-third of its fat, and considerable bulk ; on the other hand it is very palatable and wholesome. As the nutritious juices of meat escape from its cut surface under the action of moderate heat, it is best to confine them by coagulating the albumen, exposing them at first to intense heat, and when both surfaces are brown, to finish cooking the meat by removing it a little from the fire. As salt draws out the juices of meat when it is applied to the raw cut surface, it is best not to salt broiled or roasted meat until the albumen of the flesh is coagulated, which will be when the surface is brown ; the application of pepper has no perceptible effect on the cut surface of meat.

Fried meat preserves more of its juices, but is enclosed in a crust, more or less hard. which is difficult to digest ; by fried meat is meant **that** which is immersed in a quantity of smoking hot fat and quickly **cooked**, not that which has been put into a cold pan with a little fat **and** allowed to fry slowly over a poor fire ; such cooking is almost sure **to harden** meat and draw out its juices ; it is this sort of frying which overtaxes weak digestive organs.

If it is impossible to broil small cuts of meat, fry them as follows: Put a pan over the fire and let it get so hot that it will hiss when the meat touches it ; then put in the meat and brown it quickly, first on one side and then on the other, and after that finish cooking it rare or well done, seasoning it after taking it from the pan ; it will be juicy and highly flavored.

Baking has somewhat the same effect as the proper frying of meat, but the fat and juices are most perfectly preserved, because in a large joint there is a smaller cut surface exposed to the action of the heat than there is in the same bulk sliced. The effect of a cool oven is undesirable for many reasons; the slow heating of any moist food tends to promote decomposition, and sometimes meat is actually spoiled, that is, apparently tainted by being cooked in a slow oven ; even if the meat is not spoiled the low temperature tends to draw out the juices, especially if there is any water in the pan with the meat. When it is necessary to bake meat, have the oven very hot; brown the meat all over quickly, and then moderate the heat until the meat is cooked to the required degree.

An important point to be considered in the baking of meat is the ventilation of the oven. It is a well-known fact that few odors are so penetrating and enduring as those of hot or burning fats, and when these odors are retained by the iron sides of an unventilated range or stove oven, where meats are cooked, they cannot fail to impair the natural flavor and delicacy of less savory foods, such as pastry and desserts; these dishes generally call for fine manipulation and expensive materials, the effect of which is impaired and sometimes quite destroyed by having imparted to them the strong and greasy flavors harbored by the interior surface of the oven. This shows the necessity for thoroughly ventilating ovens which are used indiscriminately for meat and pastry.

Boiling is a more economical way of cooking meat than roasting, especially if soup is to be made of the pot-liquors, but as the juices of meat will escape unless the albumen of the cut surfaces is quickly coagulated, it is necessary to plunge the meat into actually boiling water in order to preserve them; the albumen once coagulated the meat may then be very gently boiled or simmered, and will be all the more tender for moderate cooking. In simmering or stewing the meat is gradually softened, and receives a wholesome addition of water, while it imparts some of its excess of nitrogenous elements to the broth, or to whatever vegetables or dumplings may be cooked with it; even a little rice boiled in pot-liquor makes a nutritious dish, the palatability of which depends upon the seasoning.

When it is remembered that before food can be digested at all it must be reduced to a soft pulp, we can see that the process of stewing is well calculated to prepare it for ready conversion into nutritive material; the addition of vegetables or dumplings to a stew increases its wholesomeness as well as its economy.

The process of braising meat is analogous to stewing, but certain peculiarities give it so much culinary superiority that it has been termed the climax of cookery. In soups and stews the solid parts of food are so saturated with fluid as to become soft and tender, the

intermediate layers of fat are either dissolved and dissipated throughout the mass of lean or mingled with the broth, from which any
excess can easily be removed; as they are semi-fluid, the nutriment
that the broth in which they are cooked draws from the meat is
preserved with them ; if they are properly made but little of it
escapes with the steam from the kettle. But it is just at this point
that the advantage of braising is apparent. The natural juices of
food assume during cooking the properties of chemical solvents when
they are equally diffused throughout the mass of the food exposed
to heat, and they impart to it a uniform flavor and consist:ncy.
In broiling, roasting, baking or stewing in any save a steam-tight
vessel, some of these juices are transformed into steam, and in that
form escape from the food, carrying with them more or less of its
nutriment; this waste is prevented in properly conducted braising.

Braising, as done in the south of France, and in some parts of
Spain, is accomplished by placing the food to be cooked in an
earthen pipkin, or a deep covered metal dish, either utensil used
having a sunken lid calculated to hold hot coals and ashes. All
braises are cooked in the same manner, the variation being in the
meats and seasonings ; when the meats are boned, the bones and
trimmings are to be placed in the bottom of the braising pan to yield
their flavor ; if the fat is abundant it may not be necessary to use it
all for the braise. At the bottom of the braising-pan the bones and
some of the fat of the meat are laid, or some slices of salt pork or
bacon ; next is placed a layer of chopped vegetables, sweet herbs,
and seasonings ; the meat is laid on these and covered with more
vegetables, and a sheet of buttered paper ; broth or hot water enough
to cover it is poured over it, the lid of the braising pan is put on and
cemented with a paste of flour and water, applied around the edges,
to prevent the escape of steam ; the pan is then placed on a thick
bed of hot coals and ashes at the side of the open fire, and the lid
covered with hot coals and ashes, or it is set in a moderate oven ; an
equal heat is then maintained for a length of time corresponding with
the size of the dish ; for instance a leg of mutton, or about seven
pounds of beef, will cook in five or six hours. As all braises should
be well cooked they are not injured by standing longer than the
time absolutely required for cooking them. Towards the close of

cooking the heat may be diminished without affecting the excellence of the dish. The fortunate possessors of a brick oven can braise to perfection. To braise on an ordinary stove the pan must be set where there is a very gentle heat ; the hot coals on the lid should be well covered with ashes, when they will retain their heat for a long time. Two large deep pans, one of which will sink down into the other about one-third of its depth, can be used for braising. Of course the gravy of the braise is strained and served with it. Definite directions for preparing several braises are given in the chapter on COOKING MEATS.

CHAPTER II.

SOUPS.

The nutritive value and palatability of soup is becoming generally understood by American housekeepers. Of course the actual nourishment of any soup depends upon the ingredients employed in making it ; but any soup offers to the hungry man an immediate and available refreshment ; in less than five minutes after soup is eaten a sensation of restored energy is experienced ; even a soup composed of vegetables or grains, with but very little animal substance, answers all the requirements of hunger. Care should be taken not to season soup too highly with salt, as this in excess decreases the facility with which the nutriment of the soup is imparted to the blood. Soup should be cooked slowly, and long enough to have all its ingredients tender. If any remains after a meal it should be cooled without being covered, except perhaps by a sieve to protect it from flies, and it should be kept in an earthen vessel, in a cool place. Below are given a few recipes for some favorite soups of a representative character.

CREAM OF SALMON.

For two quarts of soup remove the skin and bone from a cupful of cold salmon, and rub it through a fine sieve with a potato masher. After the fish is prepared make a cream soup as follows : Put over the fire in a thick, clean sauce-pan two heaping tablespoonfuls of butter and two level ones of dry flour; stir them together with a small pudding-stick until they form a smooth paste, and begin to bubble; then gradually stir in hot milk, about a half a cupful at once, until two quarts have been added to the butter and flour; stir the soup thus made until it boils; if the milk has been added gradually and well stirred the soup will be free from lumps; then stir in the salmon, prepared as directed above; let the soup boil once; season it palatably with salt, white pepper, and a very little grated nutmeg, and serve it hot. The seasoning will depend upon the taste of the fish.

Any other fish can be used, and the soup will take its name from the fish.

Or any vegetable, boiled and passed through the seive, may be added to the cream soup, which will then take its name from the vegetable.

PURÉE OF DRIED PEAS.

For two quarts of this soup peel and slice a small onion, fry it in the bottom of a soup kettle with two tablespoonfuls of butter or sweet meat drippings; while the onion is frying pick over and wash a scant cupful of dried yellow split peas; put the peas with the fried onion; add a quart of cold water and let the water slowly reach the boiling point; then place the kettle on the back part of the fire; add half a pint of cold water and let the soup boil again; add three more half-pints of cold water in this way, letting the soup slowly heat to the boiling point each time; then cover the kettle, and continue to boil the soup until the peas are tender enough to rub through a sieve with a potato masher; after the peas have been passed through the sieve return them to the soup kettle with all the soup; rub a tablespoonful each of butter and flour to a smooth paste; stir it into the soup; season it palatably with salt and pepper; let it boil once and then serve it.

Small dice of dry toast, or bits of bread fried brown in smoking-hot fat, may be served with this soup. Any dried beans or lentils may be cooked in this way.

RICE AND TOMATO SOUP.

Peel and slice a quart of fresh tomatoes, or use the canned vegetable ; put the tomatoes over the fire with a tablespoonful of butter, and fry them for fifteen minutes ; meantime pick over and wash in cold water a cupful of rice ; when the tomatoes are fried add to them enough boiling water to make two quarts of soup ; when it boils season it palatably with salt and pepper; put in the rice, and let the soup boil for twenty minutes ; then serve it hot.

BEEF BROTH WITH BARLEY.

Use for two quarts of soup two pounds of the leg of beef ; have the meat cut from the bone in one piece, and the bone well broken; put the bone in the bottom of the soup kettle ; lay the meat on it; pour in two quarts of. cold water, and let the water heat gradually; when the soup boils put in two teaspoonfuls of salt, and one teaspoonful of peppercorns or a small red pepper ; cover the kettle, and boil the soup very slowly for two hours. At the end of an hour and a half pick over half a cupful of pearl barley ; wash it in plenty of cold water, and put it over the fire in a quart of cold water; when the water boils pour it off the barley and replace it with fresh; again boil and drain the barley. When the soup has boiled for two hours take up the meat and put it aside for any dish which calls for cold boiled beef; strain the soup through a folded towel laid in a colandar, and return it to the soup kettle; remove the fat from its surface by placing several sheets of soft white paper successively on the top, removing them when they have absorbed the fat ; after the fat has been removed from the soup put in the barley and let the soup boil until the barley is just tender; then see that it is palatably seasoned, and serve it hot.

NEW ENGLAND FISH CHOWDER.

Put half a pound of sliced salt pork in the bottom of an old fashioned iron pot, and fry it brown ; when it is brown lay it on a dish, and fill the pot with alternate layers of onions and potatoes, peeled and sliced, one quart of each, and three pounds of cod or haddock cut in inch thick slices, and the fried salt pork, each layer being plentifully seasoned with salt and pepper ; pour enough cold water into the kettle to reach an inch above the top of the chowder; cover the kettle, and cook the chowder for twenty minutes ; meantime soak a pound of Boston crackers in cold water for five minutes; when the chowder is ready put in the crackers and a pint of milk; boil the chowder for five minutes, and then serve it in a tureen, with a plate of dry crackers.

CHAPTER III.

FISH AND ITS COOKERY.

Fish is exceedingly nutritious, and generally digestible, unless it is very oily ; sea-fish has the finest flavor, and is the most nourishing. Some of the best kinds, such as salmon, shad and smelt, live in both salt and fresh water. Fresh water fish are apt to be soft in fibre and muddy in taste, but these defects can be overcome to a degree by soaking them in cold salted water for two or three hours before cooking them. All kinds of fish are prime just before spawning, but should be avoided after it, because their flesh is then watery and poorly flavored. The flesh of fresh fish is quite firm, their fins are stiff, their eyes full and bright and their gills ruddy and distinct.

The salting of white fleshed fish, such as cod, haddock and shad, hardens their fibres, and destroys much of their nutriment, more of which is lost in freshening them before cooking ; rich, oily fish like eels, salmon, sturgeon, mackerel and herring, do not part with much of their nutritive value by this process, or rather they are so very nutritious that they are valuable foods despite its disadvantages.

The cooking of fish softens its fibres, coagulates its albumen, and separates the juices from the flesh, presenting them in a curd-like substance between the flakes ; this curd is most abundant in newly caught fish, and is highly esteemed by epicures. When fish is rather deficient in flavor, a little vinegar or red wine, and a few sprigs of sweet herbs cooked with it greatly improve it. Large fish for boiling should be placed over the fire in cold water and small ones in hot water; both are done when the fins pull out readily. To boil fish is the least economical way of serving it, and fish chowder the most; baked fish retains all its nutriment, and broiled fish nearly all.

Lobsters and crabs should be chosen by their brightness of color, lively movements, and great weight in proportion to their size; when lobsters are fresh the tail will flap quickly back against the body when they are lifted up. In summer the female lobster is best just before spawning, and may be known by the presence of the brownish black eggs clustered among the soft fins under the tail; if the spawn is large and abundant the flesh of the lobster has already begun to deteriorate. The male lobster is best in the winter.

HOW TO BOIL LOBSTERS.

Have ready over the fire a large pot, half full of boiling water, containing a handful of salt; when the water is actually boiling put in the lobster, head first, and boil it for about fifteen minutes, or until the shell is quite red; then take it from the boiling water, cool it enough to permit handling, and remove the flesh from the shell; throw away the soft fins which lie under the legs close to the body, the stomach which is enclosed in a sort of shell-like membrane just back of the eyes, and the intestine which runs through the middle of the tail; all the flesh of the lobster, the coral and the green fat, are to be preserved for the making of different dishes.

If the lobster is to be eaten plain boiled, make a sauce for it by mixing over the fire the coral, the green fat, two tablespoonfuls of butter, and a high seasoning of pepper and salt; pour this over the flesh of the lobster and serve it.

STEWED LOBSTER.

Boil a lobster and remove it from the shell, as directed in the preceding recipe. When the flesh is free from the shell, cut it in inch pieces and heat it in a sauce made as follows: Stir together over the fire a heaping tablespoonful of butter and a level table-spoonful of flour until they bubble; then gradually stir in a pint of hot milk; season the sauce with a level teaspoonful of salt, quarter of a saltspoonful of white pepper, and a dust of cayenne; put in the boiled lobster ; let it heat ; then stir in the yolks of two raw eggs, and serve it at once ; if the lobster boils after the egg is added the sauce will be thick and full of the cooked particles of the egg.

FRIED SMELTS.

Any small fish may be cooked after this recipe. Wash a pound of small fish in cold salted water ; draw them at the gills without splitting them, and wipe them on a dry towel ; have ready over the fire a frying-kettle, or a deep pan half full of fat ; dip the fish first in milk, then in cracker or bread crumbs, then in beaten egg, and again in the crumbs ; when the fat is smoking hot put in the fish, as many as will float, and fry them until they are golden brown; take the fish from the fat with a skimmer ; lay them on brown paper for a moment to free them from grease ; sprinkle them with salt and serve them hot.

BROILED SHA .

Any medium sized fish may be broiled this way. After the shad has been scaled and washed in cold water, split it down the back ; remove the back-bone and entrails and lay the fish between the bars of a double wire gridiron which has been well buttered ; expose the inside to the fire until it is brown and then brown the skin ; when the fish is brown on both sides lay it on a hot platter without breaking it ; spread over it a tablespoonful of butter ; season it with a saltspoonful of salt and quarter of a saltspoonful of pepper, and serve it hot.

If parsley and lemon can be obtained, chop a tablespoonful of parsley ; mix it with a tablespoonful of butter, a teaspoonful of lemon juice, a saltspoonful of salt and quarter of a saltspoonful of pepper ; use this to dress the broiled fish.

FRIED SHAD-R E.

Wash the shad-roe in cold salted water and dry it on a clean towel ; slice quarter of a pound of fat salt pork, and put it over the fire in a frying-pan and fry it brown ; when the pork is brown take it up on a hot dish and keep it hot ; put the roe into the same pan ; dust it with salt and pepper ; put a cover over the pan and let the fry for ten minutes ; then turn it over, cover it again, and fry it for ten minutes longer ; when the roe is brown lay it on brown paper for a moment to free it from fat, and then serve it with the fried salt pork.

BAKED HALIBUT, CRÈOLE STYLE.

Wash two or three pounds of halibut cut in one thick piece ; lay the fish in a deep baking-pan ; season it with salt and pepper ; put over it a quart of tomatoes peeled and sliced, and one small clove of garlic chopped very fine ; set the pan in a moderate oven, and bake the fish for about three-quarters of an hour, or until the flakes separate ; then transfer it to a hot dish ; pour the tomato over it and serve it hot.

BLUE-FISH, STUFFED AND BAKED.

Any large fish may be cooked after this recipe. After the fish has been scaled, drawn and washed in cold salted water, stuff it with the following forcemeat and sew it up ; to make the forcemeat, soak two cupfuls of bread in cold water until soft, and then squeeze out the water ; peel and chop an onion ; put it over the fire in a frying-pan with a heaping tablespoonful of butter, and fry it until it turns light yellow ; then put in the soaked bread, a level teaspoonful each of salt and marjoram, and half a saltspoonful of pepper and stir the forcemeat until it is scalding hot ; then stuff the fish and sew it up ; slice quarter of a pound of salt pork and put it into a baking-pan under and over the fish ; put a cupful of hot water in the pan ; set it in a moderate oven and bake the fish for an hour ; then remove the string used in sewing up the fish ; transfer it to a hot dish and keep it hot. Set the dripping-pan, in which the fish was baked, over the fire ; stir into it a tablespoonful of flour, and let it brown ; add enough boiling water to make a gravy of the consistency of cream ; season it palatably and serve it with the baked fish.

BOILED COD WITH EGG SAUCE.

Wash a small cod-fish, or half a large one, in cold salted water, and put it over the fire in sufficient cold water to cover it, with a handful of salt ; boil it until a fin can easily be pulled out ; then serve it with a sauce made as follows : Boil two eggs hard ; remove the shells and cut them in small dice ; put over the fire a tablespoon-

ful each of butter and flour and stir them together until they bubble ; then gradually stir in a pint of boiling water, adding it a little
at a time and stirring it in quite smoothly each time ; when the sauce
is smooth season it with a level teaspoonful of salt, quarter of a
saltspoonful of pepper and very little nutmeg ; let it boil for a
moment ; add the chopped eggs to it and serve it with the boiled cod.

Any fish may be boiled in the same way.

CHAPTER IV.

VEGETABLES AND THEIR COOKERY.

As nearly all vegetables are boiled, the temperature of boiling
water is to be considered ; this degree of heat changes certain of
their elements, and partly removes other, especially if the boiling is
too long continued ; in boiling vegetables, their albumen or casein is
hardened, the tissues softened, and the starch grains ruptured. Soft
water, well salted, is the best for boiling vegetables ; the action of the
salt is to preserve their form, color and flavor.

Green corn, string and Lima beans, peas, okra, asparagus, cauli-
flower, cabbage, Brussels sprouts, spinach and all other green and
tender vegetables are cooked in this way. After being well washed in
cold salted water they should be placed over the fire in boiling salted
water and boiled only until they are tender ; the green vegetables
should be washed in cold water as soon as they are tender, and
allowed to stand in cold water until just before using, when they are
to be heated quickly and served at once ; treated in this way their
color is perfectly preserved.

All green succulent vegetables used for salads should be very fresh
and carefully cleansed ; if they are a little wilted their freshness
can be restored by sprinkling them with water, and laying them for
several hours in a cool, dark place. Green onions, celery, cucumbers,
radishes, water-cresses, lettuce, chicory and dandelions are the best
known salad vegetables ; lettuce, which is the most popular of all,
will keep fresh several days if it is well washed in cold salted water,

wrapped in a wet cloth and laid near the ice in an ordinary refrigerator; or washed, wrapped in a wet cloth, enclosed in a tight box and kept in a cool cellar; the defective leaves must be removed and the cloth saturated with water night and morning. All green vegetables are best just before they flower, as then all their elements are fully matured and equally distributed.

The roots and tubers among table vegetables are in perfection as soon as they ripen, and they remain good until they begin to germinate if they are carefully stored in a cool, dark, dry place; at the period of germination their chemical elements are partly decomposed and concentrated at the point of the formation of the new growth; for instance, in potatoes which have begun to sprout the starch-cells are quite disorganized, and the entire substance of the tuber is watery and deficient in nutritive elements. If roots and tubers are exposed to light and air they lose more or less of their natural moisture, and become soft and shrunken; all of these are improved by being laid in cold water for an hour or more before using them. Frost-bitten vegetables should be quite submerged in cold water until the frost is withdrawn from them and forms in a thin film on their surface.

The most important of all vegetables is the potato. For general use choose heavy, even-size potatoes, with pinkish skins; for winter keeping the round varieties are preferable. Potatoes showing greenish spots near the skin have been grown too near the surface of the ground, and are less wholesome and palatable than those which are planted deep. Waxy potatoes are less palatable and digestible than mealy ones, but more hearty, because they resist the action of the digestive organs longest. The nutritive value of potatoes is not materially affected by the different ways of cooking them, unless they are wasted in peeling; when potatoes are peeled before cooking, unless they are large and very thinly pared, the waste is about one-fourth, and chiefly of their mineral elements, which lie near the skin. The analysis of potatoes boiled in their jackets shows that they contain double the quantity of the salts of potash which remains in those that have been boiled after peeling them; besides, potatoes boiled in their jackets do not waste more than an ounce in a pound. The waste in potatoes baked in their skins and eaten as soon as they are done is very small.

MEALY BOILED POTATOES.

After thoroughly washing potatoes in plenty of cold water, either with a cloth or a brush, put them over the fire in enough water to cover them, with a tablespooonful of salt to each quart of water ; the water may be either hot or cold ; the point to be remembered is to drain the potatoes as soon as they are tender enough to be pierced with a fork ; if at this point of cooking the potatoes are drained and covered with a dry towel folded several times, they may be kept hot and mealy for hours. It is the water soaking into the softened substance of the interior of the potato after it is cooked that makes it watery. If the boiled potatoes are wanted for the table directly they are tender, drain them; put the cover again on the sauce-pan in which they were boiled, and shake them about for a couple of minutes. Potatoes should be sent to the table covered with a folded napkin, because the steam condensing on the inside of the cover will fall back upon the potatoes and make them watery.

BAKED POTATOES.

If baked potatoes are served directly they are soft they are perfectly wholesome and digestible; they should never be covered except by a napkin. Breaking the skin of baked potatoes as soon as they are tender permits the steam to escape; unless this steam, which is caused by the bursting of the starch cells at the moment the potato is tender, is allowed to escape it condenses, and is absorbed by the mealy part of the vegetable, until it becomes sodden and heavy. Potatoes should always be covered with a napkin in dishing them, and baked potatoes deteriorate by standing after they are done. In a hot oven potatoes will bake in about half an hour.

TO BOIL GREEN VEGETABLES.

All green vegetables, such as globe artichokes, lettuce, asparagus, green peas, string beans, Brussels sprouts, cresses and spinach should be well washed in plenty of cold salted water; put over the fire in sufficient salted boiling water to entirely cover them, and boiled only until they are tender; then they are to be drained and laid in very cold water until wanted for the table. A few moments before the vegetables are wanted for the table, drain them and heat them very quickly with a little salt, pepper and butter; serve them as soon as they are hot.

Carrots and turnips are boiled in the same way when it is desirable to preserve their color, and subsequently heated with any sauce preferred.

GREEN CORN BOILED.

Remove the outer husks from freshly gathered green corn; turn away the tender inner folds; carefully take out the silk and turn the husks back over the ear; have ready over the fire a large pot of boiling water; put in the corn and boil it fast for about twenty minutes if the grains are full, or for a shorter time if they are small. When the corn is just tender drain it; wrap a folded napkin around it and send it at once to the table with plenty of butter, salt and pepper; or cut it from the cob, heat it quickly with butter, salt and pepper, and serve it at once.

SUCCOTASH.

Two hours before dinner wash a pound of salt pork in cold water; put it over the fire in two quarts of cold water and let it gradually boil for an hour, removing all scum as it rises; meantime shell half a peck of Lima beans, and cut the grains from twelve large ears of corn; after the pork has boiled an hour add the corn and beans and a palatable seasoning of pepper, and continue to boil the succotash for half an hour, keeping the pot covered and using enough water to prevent burning; the pork is generally served on a small platter, and the succotash in a vegetable dish. Just before dishing it see that it is palatably seasoned.

FRIED TOMATOES.

Mix on a platter two tablespoonfuls of flour, a teaspoonful of salt, and quarter of a saltspoonful of pepper; wash four large toma- toes in cold water, wipe them dry, and slice them quarter of an inch thick, laying the slices in the flour; put over the fire a large frying- pan, containing half an inch of any good fat for frying, and when the fat is smoking hot turn the slices of tomato over in the flour, put them into the pan and fry them brown on both sides, turning them carefully to avoid breaking them; dust a little salt and pepper over them, and serve them hot.

BOILED CABBAGE.

Thoroughly wash a cabbage in cold salted water; if any of the stalks seem hard and fibrous cut them out; have ready over the fire a large pot of salted boiling water, put in the cabbage and boil it only until it is tender, which will be in from fifteen to thirty minutes, according to the maturity of the cabbage; as soon as it is tender drain it, season it with salt, pepper and butter to taste, and serve it at once. Or, while it is boiling, prepare a sauce as follows: Put a tablespoonful each of butter and flour in a sauce-pan, and stir them over the fire until they bubble; then gradually stir in a pint of milk; stir the sauce thus made until it boils and is quite smooth; then season it with pepper and salt and use it for the cabbage; if the sauce is ready before the cabbage is done, keep it hot by placing the sauce-pan containing it in a pan of hot water on the stove.

FRIED PARSNIPS.

Wash six medium size parsnips in cold water; scrape off the skins, slice them lengthwise about half an inch thick; put them over the fire in a pot half full of boiling water, and boil them for half an hour; then drain them, dry them on a towel, and roll them in flour seasoned with salt and pepper. Meantime slice half a pound of salt pork and fry it brown; keep it hot on a hot dish; when the parsnips are done fry them brown in the pork drippings, which must be smoking hot when they are put into it. Serve the pork and parsnips on one dish.

FRIED ONIONS.

Peel and slice a quart of onions; put them over the fire in a frying pan containing two tablespoonfuls of butter; season them with a level teaspoonful of salt and quarter of a saltspoonful of pepper; cover the pan and let them cook for five minutes; then stir the onions so that the top layer will be changed to the bottom; again cover the pan and cook them five minutes longer, or until they are semi-transparent; then serve them on toast.

BOILED SQUASH.

If the vegetable is summer squash, and has a tender skin, it need not be peeled, but only washed in cold water and sliced; ripe summer squash and winter squash should be peeled and sliced. Have ready over the fire a pot half full of salted boiling water ; either boil the squash in the water, or steam it in a steamer set over the pot, until it is tender ; then drain it and press it in a cloth to extract all the water ; when the squash is quite free from water return it to the fire in a sauce-pan, add to it a palatable seasoning of salt, pepper and butter, stir it until it is hot, and then serve it.

CHAPTER V.

HOW TO COOK MEATS.

The principles of cooking meat have already been explained ; therefore only recipes will be given here. The directions for roasting, baking, broiling, stewing, braising, or frying, any one meat will apply to all. One point is to be remembered, *i. e.*, that salt applied to the cut surface of uncooked meat always draws out the juices, and makes it comparatively dry.

ROAST BEEF.

When the meat is brought into the house have it wiped on the outside with a clean cloth wet in cold water ; trim off any torn or defective portions, and hang the meat in a cool, dry, dark place ; do not lay it down on a board or platter, because the juice and blood which exude from it very soon taint, and are apt to spoil the entire piece of meat.

Put the meat on a spit if it is to be roasted before an open fire, or hang it in a Dutch oven, and expose it to the direct heat of a clear fire until the surface is entirely brown ; then season it with salt and pepper, and finish cooking it to the required degree. If meat is desired rare let it cook about fifteen minutes to the pound ; if medium rare, twenty to twenty-five minutes ; if well done, half an hour. If a frothed surface is desired baste the meat with the drippings in the pan every fifteen minutes while it is cooking, and dredge it with flour, seasoning it when it is brown.

When the meat is done make a gravy as directed below, using the drippings from the meat as the basis of the gravy; serve the meat when it is done to the desired degree, sending the gravy to the table with it.

BAKED MEAT.

After meat has been wiped with a wet cloth lay it in a baking-pan, set the pan in a rather hot oven, and quickly brown the meat; if enough fat does not escape from the meat to prevent burning put a tablespoonful of any good cold drippings or butter in the pan; when the meat is brown season it with salt and pepper, and occasionally baste it with the drippings in the pan; dredge it with flour in basting it, if a frothed surface is desired; when the meat is cooked to the desired degree, make a gravy as directed below, and serve it.

The effect of putting water in the pan is to draw the blood and juices out of the meat while it is cooking.

GRAVY FOR ROAST AND BAKED MEATS.

After meat has been roasted, or baked, use the drippings in the dripping-pan as the basis of a gravy; set the pan over the fire after pouring from it nearly all the fat, and leaving the thick part of the drippings in the pan; stir with the drippings a tablespoonful of flour, and brown that; then stir into the pan a pint of boiling water, adding it gradually, and stirring it until it is quite smooth; season the gravy palatably with salt and pepper, let it boil for a moment, and then serve it, with roast or baked meat.

BROILED BEEFSTEAK.

Lay the beefsteak between the bars of a buttered wire gridiron, expose it to a hot fire, and brown it as quickly as possible, first on one side and then on the other; as soon as the steak is brown remove it a little from the fire, and finish cooking it; for a steak about an inch thick allow twenty minutes to cook it medium rare, and twenty-five to thirty minutes to cook it well done. When the steak is done lay it on a hot platter, season it with salt and pepper, spread a tablespoonful of butter over it, and serve it hot

FRIED MUTTON CHOPS.

Trim the superfluous fat, and the skin from chops ; heat a frying-pan until the chops siss, on being put into it ; put the chops into the hot frying-pan, and brown them quickly, first on one side, and then on the other, and then move the pan away from the hot part of the stove, and finish cooking the chops to the desired degree. Chops fried in this way are juicy and nicely flavored ; when they are done put them on a hot platter, season them with salt, pepper and butter, and serve them hot.

STEWED VEAL.

After wiping a breast of veal with a wet cloth, cut it in pieces about two inches square ; put the veal over the fire in enough cold water to cover it, let it gradually heat, and boil gently until it is tender ; then take up the veal, and strain the broth ; put a table-spoonful each of butter and flour over the fire in a sauce-pan, and stir them until they are smoothly blended, then gradually stir in a quart of the strained broth. Season the sauce thus made rather highly with salt and pepper, put the veal into it, and let it heat ; when the veal is hot draw the sauce-pan to the side of the fire where it will not boil, stir in with the veal the yolks of two raw eggs, and serve the dish as soon as the eggs are added, being careful not to let it boil, lest the egg-yolks curdle.

BRAISED RIBS OF BEEF.

Choose a cut of the ribs of beef weighing about eight pounds ; trim away the superfluous fat, reserving enough of it to lay on the bottom of the braising-pan and over the meat ; have the rest melted for drippings ; upon the fat in the bottom of the braising-pan arrange a layer of thin slices of carrot, turnip and onion, a few sprigs of parsley, and any sweet herb except sage, a stalk of celery if it is in season, a bay leaf, a blade of mace, a teaspoonful of pepper-corns or a small red pepper, a dozen whole cloves, and a tablespoonful of salt. Lay the beef on the vegetables, put a layer of its own fat over it, pour on hot water enough to cover it ; put a sheet of buttered paper over the meat ; then put the cover of the braising-pan in place and cement it with a thick paste of flour and water, so that no steam can escape. Cover the lid of the braising-pan with hot coals and ashes, or with live coals of charcoal, and set it on the back of the range or stove, or in hot ashes by the side of an open fire, and let its contents simmer gently for four hours.   When the meat is cooked remove the paste, take off the cover of the pan, and the buttered paper, put the beef on a hot platter, while a gravy is made from a pint of the broth in which the beef was braised, a little flour browned in some of the fat from the top of the broth, and a palatable seasoning of salt and pepper.   The rest of the broth should be strained and used for sauce or soup.

CHAPTER VI.

RE-WARMED DISHES.

The art of transforming cold meats into palatable dishes is a great one, and it constitutes one of the chief excellences of French cookery.   As the limited space here can best be occupied with general directions for preparing them, only a few recipes will be given.

It should be remembered that dark meat and game should always be warmed with some brown sauce or gravy; and that fish, poultry and white meats are best with white sauces.   When acids are required, red sour fruit jellies, lemon, and claret are the proper accompaniments for the dark meats, and lemon and white wine for the white.   All warmed-over dishes should be quickly cooked, and served as soon as they are done.

Soups and Sauces to be re-warmed must first be carefully examined to make sure that they have not soured or fermented; they should then be placed in a porcelain-lined or earthen vessel, set in a pan of hot water, over the fire, and gradually heated until ready to send to the table.

Fish may be dressed the second time as flaked fish in sauce, hash, fish-cakes and puddings, sausages, omelettes, fritters, sandwiches, and pies.

Entrées, or Side-dishes, must be warmed in the same manner as soups.

MEATS are served re-warmed as *croquettes*, patties, *salmis*, curries, devils, hash, white and brown stews, scallops, *fricassées*, and in many other ways.

GAME and POULTRY can be re-warmed by seasoning the pieces highly and broiling them quickly.

VEGETABLES by no means lose their excellence at the second service. They may be warmed in any sauce or gravy, as the accompaniment of a dish of meat; or chopped and fried in butter, with pepper and salt; or minced with fish or meat, and then warmed.

COLD DESSERTS. such as bread, rice, sago, and tapioca puddings, can be sliced, dipped in beaten egg and bread-crumbs and then fried, and served with powdered sugar. Cold rice may be sweetened, made into balls, and fried, or mixed with milk, flour and egg, and fried as fritters or pancakes. Cold sago and tapioca puddings make excellent fritters, as do cold boiled oatmeal and hominy. Remember in frying to have the fat smoking hot, and to lay the fried article upon brown paper a moment after it is done, to free it from grease.

FISH BALLS.

Remove all skin and bones from a pound of any cold boiled fish, chop it fine, mix it with an equal measure of mashed potato, either hot or cold, season the mixture highly with salt and pepper, add one raw egg to it, and then form it in little balls with the hands, first wetting them slightly in cold water; roll the balls in flour seasoned with salt and pepper, put them into a frying-kettle half full of fat made smoking hot over the fire, and fry them brown; when they are done take them out of the fat with a skimmer, lay them for a moment on brown paper, to free them from grease, and then serve them.

COLD CHICKEN FRIED.

Cut cold roast, boiled or stewed chicken in pieces about two inches square; put them in a bowl, pour over them a little good table-sauce of any kind, season them with salt and pepper, and let them stand for a couple of hours, turning them over in the sauce three or four times. After two hours put the frying-kettle over the fire to heat, and make a frying-batter as follows: Mix together in a bowl a cupful of flour, the yolk of a raw egg, a level teaspoonful of salt, a tablespoonful of salad oil, and enough cold water to make a thick batter; just before frying the chicken beat the white of the egg to a stiff froth, mix it gently into the batter, dip the chicken into it, and then fry it in smoking hot fat until it is brown; take the chicken from the fat with a skimmer, lay it on brown paper for a moment, and then season it with salt, and serve it hot.

If any batter remains it can be mixed with any chopped cold meat, or with chopped apples, and fried as fritters. As the lightness of the batter depends upon the air beaten into the white of egg the latter must be used as soon 'as it is beaten, and the batter fried at once.

HUNTER'S SALMI OF DUCK.

Cut cold roast duck in rather small joints, and season them with pepper and salt; put over the fire in a shallow sauce-pan four tablespoonfuls each of salad oil, lemon juice and claret; when these ingredients are hot put in the duck, toss it about in the sauce-pan until it is hot, then put it on a dish, pour the sauce over it, and serve it hot at once.

WHITE STEW OF COLD VEAL.

Cut the cold veal in pieces about an inch square; put over the fire in a sauce-pan one tablespoonful each of butter and flour, and stir them together until they bubble; then begin to stir in boiling water, half a cupful at once, stirring this quantity smooth before more is added, until a pint has been used; stir the sauce, thus made, until it is quite smooth, season it palatably with salt and white pepper, put in the cold veal, and stir it about in the sauce until it is hot; then stir in the yolk of one raw egg mixed with half a cupful of the sauce, and serve the stew; if the sauce is allowed to boil after adding the egg it will curdle.

BROWN STEW OF COLD BEEF.

Cut cold beef in pieces about two inches square; put over the fire in a sauce-pan two heaping tablespoonfuls of sweet beef drippings or butter; when the fat is smoking hot put in the beef, and quickly brown it; when the beef is brown stir in a heaping tablespoonful of flour until it is completely mixed with the meat; then gradually add a pint of boiling water, stirring the sauce thus made until it is quite smooth ; then season it palatably with salt and pepper, add to it half a cupful of vinegar, or any good table-sauce or catsup, and let it boil gently for ten or fifteen minutes ; or until the meat is tender ; then serve it hot.

CHAPTER VII.

BREADS.

It is not difficult to make good bread if certain fixed principles are kept in mind, and some facts ; light bread is not only more palatable but actually more nourishing than that which is heavy and soggy, because it more readily permits admixture with the gastric juice, in the process of digestion. Bread is made light by the mechanical action of carbonic acid gas upon the dough ; this action is produced by the fermentation arising from the use of yeast with flour and water under certain conditions of warmth, the process being called " raising" the dough. It has been proven by scientific investigation, that the best and most nutritious bread is that which can be raised most quickly, because in prolonged raising, or fermentation, some of the nutritious elements of the flour are lost. Dough for bread can also be raised by using leaven, which is a piece of sour dough saved from one baking to the next, salt-risings, cream of tartar and soda, and baking-powder, which is a combination of the two last named ingredients with starch or rice flour.

The three first methods are usually slow, owing to the quantity of yeast or leaven employed, and more or less of the nutriment in the flour is destroyed by fermentation ; in using cream of tartar and soda, or any baking-powder, the carbonic acid gas is generated as soon as the water used for moistening the dough unites with them ; this dough must be baked before the gas escapes, otherwise the bread or biscuit will be heavy ; in using this process very little nutriment is lost from the flour.

The best flour for bread is made from what is called winter wheat; the flour has a slight yellowish tint; when a little of it is pressed in the palm of the hand it retains the marks of the skin after the pressure is removed; if mixed with water it absorbs more than fine white flour, and forms a tough elastic dough, from the quantity of gluten it contains. Fine white flour, which is nearly all starch, does not make the best bread; it looks white and tastes well, but is less nutritious than that made from a stronger and darker flour. Below are given directions for making bread by these different methods.

HOME-MADE BREAD, SLOW PROCESS.

For two loaves of medium size use three and a half pounds of flour, reserving half a pound for kneading; put three pounds of flour in a bread-pan or wooden bowl, make a hollow in the centre, without exposing the bottom of the pan; put into this hollow a pint of lukewarm water, a heaping teaspoonful of salt, and a gill of good yeast; mix with the water and yeast enough of the flour to make a thick smooth batter; gradually mix in the rest of the flour, working the dough with both hands until it is soft and smooth; ' then gather it from the pan, dust flour under and over it, cover it with a thick towel folded several times, and place the pan where no cold draughts can lower the temperature of the dough. Sometimes only part of the flour is mixed with the yeast and water, the remainder being left around the sides of the pan to protect the sponge, or thin batter or dough from the air. Usually this dough or sponge is set to rise at night, and is light enough in the morning to knead and prove, before baking; this lightness is shown by the presence of innumerable bubbles of the gas which penetrate every portion of the dough, making it porous or "light." By increasing the quantity of yeast the process of raising the bread is hastened, but care should be taken to avoid using yeast enough to make it bitter.

When the dough is light, turn it out on a floured bread board, and work or knead it with the hands, using flour enough to prevent it sticking to them, for fifteen minutes; then form it in two loaves, put them in buttered pans, cover the pans with a folded towel, and place them near the stove to rise to twice their volume; then prick the loaves two or three times with a fork, brush them with melted butter or milk, and bake them in a moderately hot oven, taking care that they do not burn. To ascertain if the bread is done run a knitting-needle or a small knife-blade into the centre of the loaf; if it has no dough or moisture on it when it is withdrawn the loaf is properly cooked. If a hard crust is desired let the bread cool without covering it; if it is wanted soft wrap it in a towel until it is cool

Sometimes in warm, damp weather bread-dough or sponge will sour before it is sufficiently light; in that case when the dough is light dissolve a saltspoonful of baking-soda in half a cupful of lukewarm water, and thoroughly incorporate it with the dough during the kneading process, using a little additional flour; only enough soda should be used to correct the acidity of the dough; and, as already directed, it must be very carefully mixed with the dough, or it will show throughout the bread in yellowish spots after it is baked.

HOME-MADE BREAD, QUICK PROCESS.

For two medium size loaves of bread use three pounds of flour, reserving a quarter of a pound for kneading; dissolve one small cake of compressed or German yeast in one cupful of lukewarm water, put it into an earthen bowl and mix with it flour enough to form a batter which will for a moment hold a drop from the mixing spoon; cover the bowl with a folded towel, place it near the fire, in some place where it is possible to bear the hand, and let it rise until it is full of little holes, or about twice its original volume; this will be in about half an hour; then add another cupful of lukewarm water containing a teaspoonful of salt, and enough more flour to make a soft dough; turn this out on a floured board, and knead it for five minutes, using sufficient flour to prevent the hands being moistened with the wet dough; when the dough is properly kneaded divide it in two loaves, put them in buttered pans, cover them with folded towels and set them near the stove to rise to twice their volume. When the loaves are light bake them in a quick oven, according to the directions given in the preceding recipe.

This preparation of dough can be baked in the form of biscuit or rolls, a tablespoonful of melted butter being stirred into the dough before kneading it; the little rolls may be brushed with a teaspoon-

ful of sugar dissolved in milk to make them glossy, before taking
them from the oven.

SALT-RISINGS BREAD.

This bread is very white, moist, and sweet, somewhat resembling
baking-powder bread, and is useful for those emergencies when yeast
cannot be obtained ; but it is less nutritious than quick homemade
bread, because the process of fermentation is prolonged. To make
it, put a pint of boiling water into a two-quart pitcher, with a teaspoonful each of salt and sugar, and a saltspoonful of soda, and let
the pitcher stand on the table until its contents are cool enough to
permit the hand to be placed in them without burning it. Then beat
in sufficient flour to form a batter thick enough to hold a drop from
the mixing spoon ; set the pitcher in a kettle of water just warm
enough to bear the hand without burning, cover the pitcher with a
folded towel, and keep the water at this temperature until the batter
is foaming and has risen to twice its original height. This may be
three or four hours. When the batter is properly risen, mix with it
flour enough to make a soft dough, and knead it as directed above,
for five minutes ; then form it into loaves, put them into buttered
pans, let them rise until their volume is doubled, and then bake them
like other loaves.

SODA BREAD.

Sift together three times, two pounds of flour, a heaping teaspoonful each of salt and baking-soda, and two heaping teaspoonfuls of
cream of tartar. Have ready two iron bread-pans well buttered, and
see that the oven is hot ; then quickly rub or chop into the flour a
tablespoonful of lard or butter, and mix it to a soft dough with a
pint of cold milk or water. Work as fast as possible ; the success
of bread of this kind depends upon the rapidity with which it is
mixed and baked.

BISCUITS.

Biscuits are made like soda-bread : or, two heaping teaspoonfuls
of baking-powder are sifted with a level one of salt, and a pound of
flour, and then they are finished as the bread is, except that they are
baked in small bits instead of in loaves.

More butter or lard is used with biscuit than with bread, and milk is generally liked for mixing them.

In general bread-making, various additions are at the discretion of the cook. Sometimes potatoes, boiled and mashed, are mixed with the dough or sponge of bread; they make the bread more solid and moist, but do not increase its nutriment. Lard, butter, sugar, and milk, are used at discretion; but it is generally believed that bread made simply with flour, salt, water, and the "raising" agent, is the most palatable and wholesome.

CHAPTER VIII.

SIMPLE DESSERTS.

A good pie seems to be the ideal dessert of the average American. The basis of all good pies is pastry, not too rich, quickly and delicately made. The following recipe will be found to yield good results, if it is carefully put into practice. In making pastry remember to use the best butter, to work quickly, and to touch it as lightly and as little as possible, keeping it cool. In summer the pastry-board may be set on two dripping-pans full of chopped ice, and ice-water used for wetting the flour.

PLAIN PASTRY.

Put in a bowl one pound of flour, and a teaspoonful of salt; chop into the flour a quarter of a pound of butter, cutting it in little flakes; then mix with the flour enough cold water to make a paste which can be rolled out without sticking to the board; use a knife for mixing the paste, in order to avoid heating it with the hand; and when it is mixed, touch it as lightly and quickly as possible, and do not press upon it except with the rolling pin; the pressure of the hand makes it heavy; when the pastry is rolled out cut another quarter of a pound of butter in large flakes, lay them over the pastry, dust them with flour, and fold the edges of the pastry inward so that the butter is enclosed at the edges; then double the pastry together so that the butter is entirely hidden, and roll it out quickly, three times as long

as it is wide; fold it in three layers, and again roll it out; repeat
this rolling and folding several times, and then use the pastry. Remember in rolling, it not to rest the hands upon it, not to press it, to
work quickly, and to keep it as cool as possible.

SLICED APPLE PIE.

Prepare a nice pastry as directed in the preceding recipe, and line
a pie-plate with it; peel and slice about six apples of medium size,
cutting away all the core; put the sliced apples high in the middle
of the pie-plate, put over them two heaping tablespoonfuls of sugar,
or more if the apples are tart, a teaspoonful of powdered cinnamon,
and a tablespoonful of butter; wet the edges of the under crust, lay
the upper crust lightly on the pie, taking care not to press the edges
to make them heavy; cut several small places in the upper crust,
brush it over with beaten egg, and bake the pie in a moderate oven
until the crust is nicely browned, and the apple tender; sift powdered sugar over the top, and use it hot or cold.

SQUASH PIE.

Peel a medium size squash, cut it in two-inch pieces, put it over
the fire in salted boiling water, and boil it until it is soft enough to
rub through a sieve with a potato masher; drain the squash before
rubbing it through the sieve; when the squash is ready, beat six eggs
with half a pound of sugar, add to them a quart of milk, two teaspoonfuls of powdered cinnamon, and the squash; mix them thoroughly, see that they are palatably sweetened and flavored, and
then use the mixture to fill pie-plates lined with good pastry; for
squash pies only an under crust is used, a half-inch strip of pastry
being laid around the edge of the crust to form a wall for holding
the squash; if, while the pie is baking the crust seems in danger of
burning, a circular strip of paper may be laid over it; the pie will be
done as soon as the squash is firm, and the under crust slightly brown.

RASPBERRY PIE.

Make a nice pastry as already directed, and line a pie-plate with
it; carefully pick over a quart of raspberries and half a pint of currants for each pie; put the fruit into the lined pie-plate, put over it a
cupful of sugar, and then cover it with pastry, wetting the under

crust near the edge to make the upper crust adhere to it; do not press the edges of the pastry; after the upper crust is laid on the pie curve the forefinger of the right hand, and press with it just inside the edge of the upper crust, making a deep groove in it; in this groove make three or four cuts in the upper crust, to permit the fruit juice to run into the groove; this will prevent it boiling out of the pie; when the pie is covered cut several places ne.. the centre of the upper crust, dust a little sugar over it or brush it with beaten egg, and then bake it in a moderate oven until the crust is nicely browned. Serve the pie hot or cold.

Other fruit pies may be made in the same way, varying the quantity of sugar to suit the flavor of the fruit.

BAKED APPLE DUMPLINGS.

Make a good pastry as already directed, roll it out about quarter of an inch thick, and cut it in pieces about five inches square, or large enough to admit of lapping the corners up over a medium size apple; peel and core as many apples as there are pieces of pastry; set an apple on each piece, fill the cores with sugar, half a saltspoonful of cinnamon, and a piece of butter as large as a grain of coffee; lap the corners of the crust up over the apples, slightly wetting them to make them adhere, brush them with beaten egg, and bake them for about half an hour, in a moderate oven, or until the crust and apple are done. Then serve them with good hard sauce.

HARD SAUCE FOR PUDDINGS.

Use equal parts of butter and sugar; beat them to a cream, flavor them with any essence preferred, or with the grated rind and juice of a lemon, and use the sauce when desired.

BOILED APPLE DUMPLINGS.

Remove the membrane from half a pound of suet, and chop it fine; sift together a pound of flour, a teaspoonful of salt, and two teaspoonfuls of baking-powder, and mix it with the chopped suet; pare and core half a dozen apples; mix the flour and suet to a paste with cold water, roll it out quarter of an inch thick, and cut it in squares of about five inches, large enough to wrap the apples in; put a teaspoonful of sugar, and half a saltspoonful of powdered spice in each apple, wrap the paste up around them, and tie them in little pudding-cloths ; the cloths must first be dipped in scalding hot water and then thickly dusted with flour before wrapping the dumplings in them ; work quickly, and when all the dumplings are ready put them into a large pot or sauce-pan half full of boiling water, and boil them steadily for one hour ; then turn them out of the cloths, and serve them hot with sauce.

CREAM PUDDING SAUCE.

Mix together in a sauce-pan over the fire one tablespoonful each of butter and flour until they bubble ; then gradually add a pint of milk, stirring all the time, and keeping the sauce free from lumps ; when all the milk is used put into the sauce four tablespoonfuls of sugar, and a teaspoonful of any flavoring preferred ; let the sauce boil once, and then use it.

RACKET CLUB PUDDING.

Make a custard of the yolks of four eggs, quarter of a pound of sugar, and a quart of milk ; slice a loaf of stale bread ; pick over and wash half a pound of dried currants ; put the bread and currants in layers in a buttered earthen dish, pour the custard over them slowly, so that all of it may be absorbed by the bread , then bake the pudding in a moderate oven for half an hour. When the pudding is done whip the whites of the eggs to a stiff froth ; gently stir with the beaten whites four tablespoonfuls of powdered sugar, and lay them on the pudding ; return it to the oven a moment to slightly color it, and then serve it hot.

CREAM RICE PUDDING.

Pick over four ounces of rice, wash it in two waters, put it into a baking-dish with three ounces of sugar and a teaspoonful of flavoring, pour in three pints of milk, and put the pudding into a moderate oven to bake for an hour and a half, taking care that it does not burn.

CUMBERLAND PUDDING.

Remove all membrane from six ounces of suet, and chop it fine ; pick over, wash, and dry on a clean towel, six ounces of dried currants ; pare, core, and chop six large apples ; cut four ounces of citron in thin slices ; grate the rind of one orange and one lemon, and squeeze the juice in separate cups ; put all these ingredients except the lemon-juice into a mixing bowl ; add to them six ounces of dry bread crumbs, six eggs, six ounces of sugar, and a teaspoonful of salt, and mix them thoroughly. Butter a pudding mold, put in the pudding, place the mold in a sauce-pan containing sufficient boiling water to reach two-thirds up the sides of the mold, set it over the fire, and steam the pudding for three hours. Then turn it from the mold, dust it with powdered sugar, and serve it with rum sauce.

RUM SAUCE.

Melt together over the fire two ounces of sugar, a gill of boiling water, and the juice of one lemon ; add one gill of the best Jamaica rum, and serve the sauce.

SOFT GINGERBREAD.

Prepare a cake-pan lined with buttered paper. Melt one ounce of butter, stir it into half a pint of molasses, with one level teaspoonful each of ground cloves, cinnamon and ginger ; dissolve one level teaspoonful of soda in half a pint of boiling water, mix this with the molasses, and very quickly stir in half a pound of sifted flour; pour this batter into the cake tin, and bake it at once in a moderate oven for about half an hour, or until you can run a broom splint into it and withdraw it clean, *i. e.*, free from moisture. If the broom splint is damp or clogged with cake dough, be sure that the gingerbread is not done. Do not take it from the oven until it is done.

GOLD CAKE.

Line a cake pan with buttered paper. Sift together one cupful of flour, one teaspoonful of baking-powder, and a saltspoonful of salt. Beat two heaping tablespoonfuls of butter to a cream with half a pound of granulated sugar ; beat the yolks of six eggs to a cream ; stir into the butter and sugar two-thirds of a cupful of milk, and a cupful of flour *not mixed with the baking-powder;* then stir in the yolks of the eggs ; when all these ingredients are ready quickly add the cupful of flour with which the baking-powder is sifted ; add also a teaspoonful of vanilla extract, put the cake at once into the pan lined with buttered paper, and bake it in a moderate oven for about half an hour, or until a broom splint run into the centre can be withdrawn clean.

SILVER CAKE.

Proceed as directed in the recipe for Gold Cake, substituting the whites of six eggs beaten stiff, for the yolks, and almond flavoring for the vanilla.

SPICE CAKE.

Slice two ounces of citron ; pick over and wash a cupful of dried currants, and rub them dry on a towel ; remove the stones from a cupful of raisins ; butter a cake-pan, or line it with buttered paper. Beat to a cream one cupful of butter and two cupfuls of brown sugar ; beat three eggs to a foam, and stir them with the butter and sugar ; add half a pint of cold water, two teaspoonfuls of powdered cinnamon, half a teaspoonful of powdered cloves, and half a nutmeg grated ; sift three and a half cups of flour with one teaspoonful of salt, and two of baking-powder, stir the flour into the cake mixture, quickly add the fruit, put the cake into the buttered pan, place it in a moderate oven, and bake it until a broom splint can be run into it and withdrawn without sticking.

LEMON SNOW.

Soak an ounce of gelatine in a pint of cold water for half an hour ; peel the yellow rind from three lemons, and squeeze their juice ; put both juice and rind into a sauce-pan over the fire with half a pound of sugar and the soaked gelatine, and stir them until both are dissolved ; then strain them into a bowl and let them partly cool ; meantime beat the whites of three eggs to a stiff froth, and then beat them with the other ingredients ; pile the lemon snow, thus made, high in the middle of a glass dish, and serve it cold.

CHAPTER IX.

TABLE TALK.

DINNER GIVING.

The pleasantest dinners are those where the hostess suffers no anxiety, where every dish is perfection of its kind, and where no awkward mistakes are made by the attendants. So much of the comfort of a dinner depends upon the service that the attendants should know what they are expected to do, and be familiar with the house and its appliances ; they should move quietly and keep cool.

A few sensible and practical rules will serve for the guidance of inexperienced hosts ; and by following them even a novice can give pleasant entertainments.

1. Give dinners within your means.

2. Do not make experiments. Either serve the dishes in which you excel, or hire a good cook to give you a variety.

3. Never apologize for a dish. If it is not good keep it off the table.

4. Always invite people of congenial tastes and friendly feelings.

5. Do not give large dinner parties if you want your guests to enjoy themselves.

Attention to these points, and polite consideration for the peculiarities of your guests will soon make you an accomplished host.

TABLE DECORATIONS.

There is no branch of household art where taste can be more finely displayed than in the arrangement of the table. A spotless cloth, clear glasses, and shining cutlery, feast the sight before the substantial meal begins, and they are within the reach of every one. A cheerful dining-room, sunny by day, and well lighted by night, and a neat and well ordered table are most attractive ; the simplest

materials will shape themselves under deft fingers in beautiful deco-
rations. If it is impossible to brighten the table with a few flowers,
or a pretty bit of china, it is easy to place the various dishes of food
upon it in a symmetrical manner. It takes no more tir to lay a
table properly than to throw the dishes at it. The operation only
demands the exercise of a little forethought and memory. Every
cover should be laid with knife, fork, spoon, glass, bread, salt, and a
napkin; and unless the table is closely attended, *carafes* or pitchers
of cold water should be placed upon it where all can reach them.

THE DINNER SERVICE.

A dinner service consists of a covered soup-tureen and ladle and
deep plates for soup, platters and plates for fish and meats, deep covered dishes for vegetables, a gravy-tureen, salad bowl, cheese tray,
sauce-boat, and a pudding dish, with small plates for dessert; the
salad and cheese are usually served with, or directly after the roast.
These sets of dishes can be bought in New York from five dollars up,
according to style and quality. Unless a person is rich enough to at
once replace broken dishes belonging to decorated sets, plain white
dishes are most desirable; they are in perfect taste, and with a snowy
cloth, and clean glassware, they set a table nicely.

MENUS, OR BILLS OF FARE.

The custom of providing bills of fare for each guest at table is a
pleasant and convenient one. Little cards are made called *menu*
cards, with flowers or ornamental designs upon one side, enclosing a
space for the name of the guest who is to occupy the place where
they are laid upon the table, the bill of fare being written upon the
reverse. They are made of smooth pasteboard, upon which writing
can be done with ink.

Large *menu* cards, about four inches by six square, are sometimes
preferred, especially when wine is to be used; the wines accompany-
ing the different courses are specified with them upon the *menu* cards.
When these large cards are used it is not necessary to provide one
for every guest.

When flowers are plentiful it is a pretty custom to place a little
bunch at the place for each guest, those for gentlemen being tiny,
and the ladies' bouquets being tied with ribbons.

THE ENGLISH DINNER SERVICE.

In the service of dinner after the English fashion, the table must be laid with two or three cloths, the under one being of delicately tinted or figured damask, called the dessert cloth; as many cloths are used as there are courses at the dinner; as each course is finished the attendants remove everything from the table, gather up the top cloth, and take it away; they then lay the table freshly for the second course; sometimes in a dinner of three courses the white upper cloth serves for two, and is then removed to give place to the dessert, thus making only one change necessary.

In this division of the dinner into courses, several dishes are placed on the table at once, the largest ones before the host and hostess, to be carved by them and placed on plates, which are passed from their left hand by the waiters, to the left hand of the guests. The soup, salad, and large sweets are set before the hostess, and the other large dishes before the host, unless two of the same sort are served at once, when one is put before each. One disadvantage of this kind of service is that when more than one joint or large dish is used some are apt to grow cold before they are served. And, besides, it makes carving a necessary accomplishment both to the host and hostess.

In such a dinner as the following there would be three services or courses; all the dishes included in each one being put upon the table at the same time:

FIRST COURSE.
Oysters on the Shell.

Julienne Soup.   Cream of Celery.

Filets of Sole, Tartar sauce.

Braised Rack of Mutton.   Game Pie.

Relishes.

SECOND COURSE.
Roast Poultry.   Roast Game Birds.

Salad of Lettuce.

Spinach with Cream.   Green Peas.   French Beans.

THIRD COURSE.
Fruit Tarts.   Lemon Jelly.   Cabinet Pudding.

Cheese.   Nuts.   Fruit.

Coffee.

THE DINNER À LA RUSSE.

The Russian style of serving dinner has of late years grown rapidly in favor, both because of the attractive possibilities of the table service, and the relief from carving which it affords the host.

In arranging the bill of fare for a dinner *à la Russe*, the hostess can select such dishes as can easily be carved in the kitchen or at the side table by the servants, and then passed to the guests, beginning with the guest at the right hand of the host, passing to the other extreme of the table, to the hostess, and back on the other side to the host; the plate of the hostess should not be removed until the guests have finished eating. In this service between each course a plate with a knife and fork laid on it, is placed before each guest by the waiter; the guest should at once lay the knife and fork upon the table. The waiters do not necessarily wear white gloves, but they should have fine napkins in the right hand, the thumb of the hand being so covered with the napkin that it does not touch the plate; of course the hands should be scrupulously clean.

In the Russian dinner, an *épergne,* or low dishes of flowers occupy the middle of the table, and about the board are arranged pretty dishes containing olives, small relishes, and sweets, fruit, nuts, confectionery, and sweet biscuit; these trifles, with pretty *bouquets* and *boutoniéres,* of bright colors and pleasant odors, add new charms to the pleasantest of all repasts.

With well trained servants a dinner *à la Russe,* or a medium number of dishes, need not occupy more than two hours. The following is a fair *menu,* which is available at almost any season.

FIRST COURSE.
Oysters, or Little Neck Clams, on the Shell.
Potage à la Reine.
Bass, *à la Chambord.*
Potatoes, with *Hollandaise* Sauce.

SECOND COURSE.
Filet of Beef, larded, *à la Macedoine.*
Macaroni, *au Gratin.*   Rice *Croquettes.*

THIRD COURSE.
Lobster Cutlets.   French Peas.   Spinach *purée.*

FOURTH COURSE.
Roast Duck, with Currant Jelly.
Salad, with French Dressing.
Roquefort Cheese.

FIFTH COURSE.
Charlotte *Russe.* *Diplomatique* Pudding.
Candied Fruit. Confectionery.
Coffee.

AMERICAN DINNER SERVICE.

A third form of service, preferred personally, as combining all the advantages of the two already given, and still preserving the genial element of individual hospitality, has been considered the most delightful way of serving a dinner, by many guests.

The table is laid as for the dinner, *à la Russe,* with the relishes, small sweets, and confectionery ; the oysters at each place ; the first course of soup and fish are placed before the host and hostess, and served by them, the waiters taking up each plate as it is served, and placing it before the guest ; at the same time, with the fish, passing the potatoes.* In the succeeding courses the same method is followed, until the dessert is reached, the cloth being cleared from crumbs, and all the glasses except those for water, champagne, and madeira, sherry, or port ; only one of these wines is taken with dessert. Coffee is served in the drawing-room directly after dinner ; and tea in an hour to the guests who remain.

FIRST COURSE.
Oysters on the Shells.
Consommé. Salmon, with Shrimp sauce.
Parisienne Potatoes.
Relishes.

SECOND COURSE.
Salmi of Duck, with Olives. Lobster Salad.
French Beans. Asparagus with Cream.
Oyster Patties.
ROMAN PUNCH.

THIRD COURSE.
Roast Chicken, with Potato *Croquettes.*
Game Birds with Salad.
Green Peas. Cheese Straws.

FOURTH COURSE.

Charlotte of Strawberries.   Orange *Croquante.*
Panachée Jelly with Fruit.
Confectionery.   Candied Fruit.
Coffee.

None of these dishes are difficult to carve or serve, a point which should always be heeded; and placing them (with the exception of the vegetables) upon the table, adds greatly to the home-like aspect of the dinner.

WAITING AT THE TABLE.

When the carving is done at the table in this way, the duty of the attendants is lightened; the dishes are brought to the pantry by the cook or kitchen maid; the wine and all the table service required are placed upon the side-table, and all accessories to the dinner are in the room, so that the waiters need never leave it; two can easily attend a dozen or more guests. This routine is easily followed; it prevents all confusion, and suits a simple dinner or an elaborate one.

DINNER ETIQUETTE.

The planning of the dinner being attended to, the hostess should be dressed and in the parlor at least fifteen minutes before the dinner hour, to receive her guests. Her station should be near the door, where she can greet each new comer with a pleasant word, and chat a little, if there is time between the arrivals. As the gentlemen enter they may receive a *boutoniére* and an envelope containing the name of the lady they are expected to take to the table; if they are not acquainted they should so inform the hostess at once, in order that the introduction may take place without delay. Guests seated by each other at table should chat without the formality of an introduction, if they are strangers; this does not involve a subsequent recognition without mutual consent. The most distinguished gentleman present always escorts the hostess; the host leads the way to the dining-room with the lady who is the guest of honor, the other guests follow, generally without precedence in this country, and the hostess comes last with her escort; the host has, of course, previously so arranged the seating of the guests that every one has a congenial neighbor; all may be seated as soon as they enter the room and find the places designated for them by the name on their *menu* card. The host places the chief lady guest upon his right, and the escort of the hostess takes the seat of honor at her right hand. When all are seated, if there are oysters upon the table they may be eaten at once.

Dinner-table talk should be the occupation of the hour; the dinner itself only the accompaniment of agreeable and entertaining conversation. When the dinner is well arranged, so that the attendants can manage it, the hostess can devote herself to the pleasure of her guests; she should avoid giving noticeable directions to the servants; and if any delay or mischance occurs she should not appear to see it. A word about serving the guests. The guest of honor, or the oldest lady at the table should be served first, then the other ladies; and finally the gentlemen.

When the dinner is over the hostess should bow to the most distinguished lady present, who should rise and leave the room, the host opening the door, the other ladies following her as they happen to be seated, and the hostess going last. It is only a graceful attention on the part of the gentlemen that they should rise, and remain standing, while the ladies leave the room; they may then, if they wish, return to the table with the host for coffee, or follow the ladies into the drawing room, and take it there with them. When the ladies reach the parlor the hostess should give a few moments conversation to each; and is at liberty to ask any one to sing or play, or she may omit this without social offence. Any guest who is asked to entertain the others should do so at once, unless there is some definite reason for declining.

The host remains in the dining-room with the gentlemen, for coffee and cigars, for about half an hour. All then join the ladies; and tea may be served, or not, as the hostess elects.

If strict etiquette is followed no guest must leave until the guest of honor has departed; then others may go without precedence, after expressing to the hostess their appreciation of the pleasant evening.

The card etiquette of dinners is definite; if the guest is a lady, who has previously been a stranger to the hostess, she may simply leave a card the next day, or certainly not later than the third day;

or the acquaintance may be pursued. If she is an intimate friend, a call within a couple of weeks is all that is required. In the country, where one cannot always get about easily, a call within any reasonable time is permissible.

A dinner invitation should be accepted or declined without delay. Dinner invitations should be accepted only from those whose friendship one desires to retain, and should always be returned, in kind, within the season. Punctuality at dinner is imperative. The sending of a card by post is scarcely a courteous acknowledgment of a dinner invitation ; a call is the proper courtesy. Of course when one is not keeping house, dinner obligations must be returned by some other form of social entertainment.

CHAPTER X.

HINTS FOR THE LAUNDRY.

The manual labor of washing is so hard that every hint concerning ways of saving unnecessary work is important. Much mechanical ingenuity is devoted to the construction of labor-saving appliances, and the nearest dealer in house-furnishing goods can always afford full information concerning them ; only the most ordinary articles will be mentioned here, because this chapter is designed for the use of some persons who may be unable to procure the so-called "latest improvements"; results will be all the better if they are available.

CONDITION OF UTENSILS.

The first care is to see that every utensil employed in laundry work is in proper order. The tubs should be clean, and free from nails upon which the clothes could catch during the washing ; in dry weather they should be kept partly filled with water to prevent shrinking ; if a little perforated shelf can be fitted against one side, near the handle, it will be found very useful for holding the soap, which does not always remain upon the wash-board. The wash-board should be free from nails, or rough places, which might tear the clothes. The wash-bench should be firm and steady, and high enough to obviate any unnecessary fatigue in bending over the tubs.

The wash-boiler should always be rinsed out and wiped dry while it is warm ; if any part of it becomes rusty the clothes should be enclosed in an old sheet for boiling, to avoid spotting them with iron-rust ; wash-boilers do not need scouring ; washing and drying them while they are hot cleanses them perfectly, while scouring increases their liability to become rusty.

CLOTHES-LINES AND PINS.

Lines of cotton or hemp are better than wire or galvanized lines of any kind ; but these lines should always be taken down as soon as the washing is over, or they will collect dust and soil the clothes hung upon them. In the country a closely clipped hedge, or a clean grass-plot is excellent for drying and bleaching clothes.

Clothes-pins should be of wood ; and they should always be put into a special bag or basket, as soon as they are taken from the line to keep them clean and avoid loss.

WATER FOR WASHING.

Soft water is better than hard for washing, and clean rain water the best of all ; when hard water is boiled a deposit of its mineral elements, notably of chalk, is made upon the sides and bottom of the boiler ; every grain of chalk in water used for washing destroys about ten times its weight in soap before a lather can be raised, and the semi-solid compound formed by the action of hard water on soap clogs the texture of the clothes. The fact that the mineral elements of hard water are deposited by boiling indicates that it should be boiled before using it for washing ; putting clothes into it while it is cold, and letting them boil in it, fixes both the chalk and the dirt in their fabric, and so discolors them, and makes them harsh and stiff.

CHEMICALS FOR SOFTENING WATER.

Some mineral elements cannot be deposited by boiling, notably the sulphate of lime ; in such case a little soda or borax boiled in the hard water will tend to soften it. When soda is used to soften water, or to facilitate the removal of dirt from clothes in washing, they should be well rinsed in clear water to ensure its entire removal, or the fabric will be injured, and a yellowish tinge will appear on it when it is exposed to heat. Borax, which has the property of softening hard water, does not injure the most delicate fabric; it may be used in the proportion of a tablespoonful to about two gallons of water.

Pearlash and lye, both made from wood ashes, are not now used in washing, because soda and borax answer their purpose. The various washing crystals, and bleaching powders, all contain more or less soda and lime, and are all injurious to clothes. If they are ever used to remove stains they should be thoroughly rinsed out of the fabric upon which they are employed.

SOAP.

It is true that soda enters into the composition of soap, but the fat in the soap neutralizes its corrosive action so that it does not injure fabrics. Soap newly made contains more or less water; this makes it dissolve readily in water, and waste rapidly. As even the best soap contains some water it is best to buy it in advance of use, and dry it in pieces of convenient size. Cheap soap contains such an excess of water that its economy is very doubtful.

STARCH.

The ordinary starch of the stores will answer very well for laundry-work if it is properly made. Quarter of a pound of dry starch will make two quarts of liquid starch. To prepare it for use have ready three pints and a half of boiling water; put into a tin pan, or an open sauce-pan, quarter of a pound of starch; with a wooden spoon gradually add a scant pint of cold water, and then not quite half a pint of hot water, stirring the starch all the time; then stir in the three pints of boiling water, adding it by degrees, and stirring it smooth; set the sauce-pan over the fire and let the starch boil for quarter of an hour; a tablespoonful of salt, a lump of loaf sugar, or a small piece of wax or of spermaceti candle, stirred with the starch until dissolved, or melted in it, will make it smooth, and prevent it sticking to the iron; starch should be stirred while it is boiling, and then strained, and set aside to become cool enough to use, a plate being placed over it to prevent the formation of a scum upon the surface.

When articles are to be starched, only enough starch is to be used to saturate them; instead of dipping them into the vessel of starch, put a little of it into another one and rub them in it.

Flour starch is often used for the coarser pieces of the washing. Potato starch will also serve for such purposes.

Potato starch is made by grating peeled potatoes into a pan of water, stirring the pulp well, and then quickly pouring both water and pulp into a sieve to drain; if this operation is quickly performed the starch of the potato will be carried through the sieve with the water, and will settle at the bottom of the bowl into which it is allowed to drain; when the starch has settled pour the water carefully off from the top, without disturbing the starch, and replace it with clean water; let the starch settle, and again change the water; change it as many times as is necessary to leave the water free from the yellowish hue first imparted by the potato pulp. When the water seems clear pour it off the starch, put the starch into a bag made of clean cotton cloth of close texture, and let it dry. To use the potato starch mix it in a large bowl with a little cold water, then pour boiling water upon it, stirring it until it is smooth; then add a very little blueing, and dip the articles which are to be starched into it while they are still wet.

LAUNDRY BLUE.

Both indigo and ultramarine are used as bases for laundry blues; the latter is considered preferable because of its clear blue tint, and because it is less likely to eventually discolor delicate white fabrics. All blues should first be dissolved in a little water, and then mixed with the rinsing water, or starch, for which they are required. The excessive use of laundry blue is to be reprobated, especially if the object be to conceal the yellowish tint caused by poor washing.

WASHING.

All soiled clothing should be washed as soon as possible, because the longer dirt of any kind remains in a fabric the harder it is to remove, and the more injury it does the fabric itself.

Stains of all kinds on clothes should be washed out before they are laid aside for the regular wash. The stains usually resulting from table use to linen will yield to soap and warm water; claret stains should be covered with salt while still wet, and then rinsed away; fruit stains yield readily to the action of chloride of lime, in the proportion of a tablespoonful to a quart of cold water, especially if a few drops of lemon-juice or vinegar are used with the lime; as soon as the stain disappears the fabric must be carefully rinsed in clear water. Metal or silver spoons and tinned utensils are injured by the lime; it should therefore be used in earthen or wooden vessels. To remove ink-stains from white cloth, wash them in cold clean water at once; then apply lemon-juice and salt, or salts of lemon, or a weak solution of muriatic acid, until the stain disappears, and thoroughly rinse the acid away with plenty of clear water. Iron-rust can usually be removed by the same method, unless the stains are a long time set in the cloth. To remove paint stains from any article that can be washed, first rub enough lard or unsalted butter into the fabric to unite completely with the paint, and then wash the grease out with soap and warm water.

Before the washing-day sort the clothes, placing all the bed linen and the cotton and linen under-clothing in one heap, the table-linen and dining-room towels in another, the flannels by themselves, and the colored hose and dresses apart; in sorting the clothes untie all strings, and unfasten all buttons and buckles; wet all soiled portions, and rub soap on them, excepting the flannels, and then put the clothes in tubs partly filled with warm water containing a little soap, and let them soak all night; the flannels must neither be soaped or soaked.

In the morning begin by adding warm soapy water to that in which the clothes were soaked over night, rub more soap on the soiled parts, and wash them well on the wash-board; as fast as they are washed wring them, and put them into more warm soapy water; after a second washing through this water the clothes may either be boiled for a few moments in suds or scalded; to boil them put them into a boiler with enough soapy warm water to cover them, place the boiler over the fire, and boil the clothes gently for fifteen or twenty minutes; fast or long continued boiling is apt to turn clothes yellow; after the clothes are scalded or boiled add a little blue water to them, and wash them through the suds; then rinse them through plenty of cold clean water, wring them as dry as possible, and hang them out. Colored muslins require extremely careful washing in two soapy waters, no soap being rubbed on them, and rinsing in clean cold water; they should be starched as soon as they are rinsed.

WRINGING OUT CLOTHES.

This is really one of the most important operations in laundry work, because unless the clothes are entirely freed from dirty water they can never look clean and white. If the clothes are to be wrung by hand they should be gathered in an even twist, and then wrung firmly, with a steady pushing and squeezing motion, until as much water is extracted as will escape under the pressure of the hands; a jerking, tearing motion injures the clothes by straining the fabric, and sometimes tearing it. The steady pressure of wringing machines is less injurious than any uncertain motion of the hands; for heavy articles, such as blankets and counterpanes, it is almost indispensable. As soon as any article is wrung out it should be shaken from the folds.

HANGING OUT CLOTHES.

After clothes have been wrung out from the rinsing water they should be hung upon the lines to dry, care being taken to place the large pieces in the middle of the lines, with the shortest side towards the wind, so that they cannot be whipped against the clothes poles by the action of the wind. Fine fabrics, such as muslins and laces, should never be hung out in windy weather, and should always have a towel or pillow-case under them to keep the line from tearing them. Clothes never should be hung by the strings; under-garments, except drawers, should be hung by the bottom; drawers, trousers, and flannels should be hung by the bands, or thickest parts.

After the clothes are hung out, all the tubs, boards, boilers, wringers, and other articles used in the washing, should be cleansed and put away until the next washing-day; and the laundry put in order for ironing.

FOLDING AND STARCHING.

When the clothes are dry they should be sorted, those for starching being laid on a clean table in the laundry; those for immediate ironing, without starching, should be sprinkled and rolled, and placed in a basket by themselves; the clothes for starching should be treated first. After the starch is made the muslins and laces should be dipped into moderately thick starch, dried, and then again dipped and dried, in the sun or near the fire; after they are dried the second time sprinkle them with clean water, and clap them between the hands until they are dry enough to iron; or spread them on a damp cloth, and roll them up, letting them lie in the cloth for two or three hours; then iron them. It has already been said that colored muslins should be starched as soon as they are rinsed after washing. Clear muslins look the better for being ironed twice, in opposite directions. Embroidered muslins and worked coarse laces should be laid wrong side up on several thicknesses of flannel, and perfectly smoothed with the hand before ironing; the thinnest parts of muslin and lace garments should be ironed first because they dry soonest; caps, collars, fichus, and aprons, where the lace is full, should have the frill ironed first, then the rest of the piece, and the frill fluted at the finish. In plaiting frills, each plait should be laid by the thread, from the hem toward the upper part, and held until ironed in place.

IRONING DRESSES.

The thickest parts of dresses, such as the waist-bands, the gathers of the skirt and sleeves, the double parts of the waist, and the heavy ruffles should be ironed first; and the plain part of the skirt the last of all; the skirt should be kept damp until ready for ironing. A skirt-board, about five or six feet long, and eighteen inches wide, covered first with blanket and then with cotton cloth, is necessary for ironing dresses nicely. Dresses should be first ironed on the wrong side, and then finished on the right.

IRONS.

The smoothing irons should be kept clean and free from rust; this can easily be done by rubbing them with a little powdered bath-brick sifted through a piece of coarse muslin, or by polishing them with fine emery paper. The heaviest that can be handled are the best for use; a rounded iron is the best for polishing starched surfaces; it should be used with a rocking, rolling motion, and considerable force; nickel-plated polishing irons are excellent, and not extravagant in cost, because they last a long time Muslins, prints, and flannels should be ironed with moderately cool irons; shirts and collars require hotter ones.

IRONING BOARDS AND BLANKETS.

The ironing table should be covered with a thick blanket, folded several times, and over that a clean, thick sheet; another cloth should be folded and laid near the iron stand, and the irons tried upon it before applying them to the clothes, to make sure that they are not hot enough to burn. Iron holders should be padded thickly enough to protect the hand from the heat of the iron.   Shirt-boards, and bosom-boards, should be covered like the ironing table; and when they are not in use they should all be protected from dust and dirt; the coverings should be washed often enough to keep them quite clean.

STARCHING AND IRONING SHIRTS.

Where collars and cuffs are attached to shirts they should be starched with thicker starch than that used for the rest of the garment, and then dried before sprinkling; the bosoms should be made very stiff; an excellent way to starch them is to lay them on a washboard, and rub thick starch into them with the hand, after that dry them, then with a damp cloth rub off all particles of starch, and dampen the entire garment to a moderate degree; spread the shirt smooth upon the table, lay the cuffs, collar, and bosom so that they do not touch each other, and roll each shirt up by itself.

For ironing shirts use heavy irons, not hot enough to scorch the cloth; iron first the thick bands, then the sleeves and bodies, and the bosoms last, being careful not to scorch the linen. If the starch sticks to the iron clean it off at once, using the bath-brick, then rub the iron smooth and clean on a piece of clean cloth, and then on another with a little beeswax rubbed on it; before again placing the iron on the linen rub it with a damp cloth to remove all rough particles of starch, and then again proceed with the ironing. To gloss the linen use the smoothing or polishing iron with the rounded edge, rubbing it forcibly over the linen, with a rocking, rolling motion.

FLANNELS.

The cause of the shrinkage of woolen fabrics is that, in rubbing, the little points of the fibres of the wool become matted and tangled together; the action of soap applied directly to the flannel, of soda, and of hard water, is similar. Flannels should never be soaked, or rinsed in clean water ; a little borax may be dissolved in water intended for washing them. Two or three strong lathers should be made, with soap and water as hot as the hands can be put into, and a little blue added to the one which is to be used last.

The flannels should be well shaken or brushed to free them as far as possible from dust and dirt, and then soused up and down in the suds ; they should then be squeezed, rather than wrung, as dry as possible, from one lather to another ; and out of the final lather they should be quickly hung, with the thickest parts up, and dried as fast as possible in the open air ; when nearly dry they should be smoothed and rolled, and then ironed with a moderately cool iron.

DIAMOND

STOVES AND RANGES

Are the best to buy, because they are the Quickest Bakers, the most Durable, and the most Economical in the consumption of Fuel.

SPLENDID BASE BURNERS

Are the most powerful Heaters, and consume less Fuel than any hard coal Base Heater ever constructed.

FURNACES.

All sizes and Styles, for Heating Dwellings and Public Buildings.

MANUFACTURED ONLY BY

FULLER & WARREN CO.

No. 56 LAKE STREET, CHICAGO.

THE GOOCH FREEZER COMPANY,

MANUFACTURERS OF

ICE CREAM FREEZERS,

109 Sycamore St., CINCINNATI, O., U. S. A.

THE GOOCH PATENT

PEERLESS & GIANT

Ice Cream Freezers.

BEST IN THE MARKET.

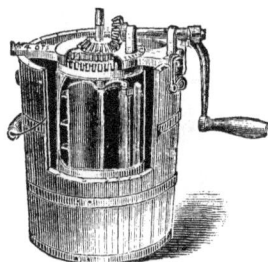

PEERLESS.

PRICE LIST.

PEERLESS.

3 Quart,	$ 4	50
4 "	5	50
6 "	7	00
8 "	9	00
10 "	12	00

GIANT.

14 Quart,	$20	00
18 "	25	00
21 "	30	00
25 "	35	00
32 "	40	00
42 "	45	00

GIANT.

THE GOOCH FREEZERS have grown into such popularity that they are now acknowledged without an equal in the market. From a limited sale on their introduction to the public, they have now reached an annual sale of Thirty Thousand. The **Peerless** is celebrated for its simplicity of construction. Perfect adaptability to its use, and the great variety of work it accomplishes, beyond the ordinary freezers. Besides its use for making the best quality of Ice Cream and Water Ices, it can be used for making Frozen Fruits, Jellies, Creams, Custards, Blanc-Mange, and Fruit Ices, making them doubly valuable in any family.

The **Giant** is especially adapted for Confectioners or Hotel use. The most decisive proof we can offer that our Freezers are superior is: Dealers are constantly taking up the sale of them, and are discarding inferior Freezers, heretofore thought good ones. We invite a careful inspection of our Freezers, and our claims for them, which accompany every Freezer. You will find them for sale by one or more dealers in nearly every city and town in the United States and Canadas. We make a broad claim that our Freezers are twice as good as any other in the market. If more convenient to you than looking them up, drop us a Postal Card and we will give the address of a dealer near you who sells our Freezers.

1863. IT STANDS AT THE HEAD. **1884.**

THE

LIGHT-RUNNING "DOMESTIC"

Is the Grandest Triumph of Sewing Machine
Mechanical Skill.

TWENTY YEARS'

PRACTICAL TEST.

(No. 4 Family Machine.)

This cut, with one of the drawers removed, shows its construction to be both strong, artistic and durable. The drawers are large, elegantly furnished. The Shelves are of Iron, and give the requisite strength, and yet are light and airy. The best Wood Work the world ever saw.

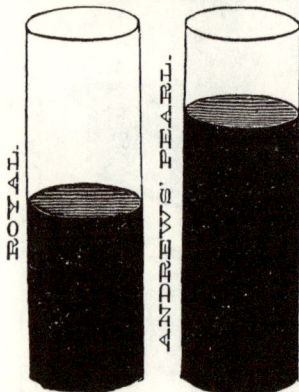